PULL-OUT MAP

The pull-out map with this book is a comprehensive street plan of the city, with a more detailed map of Central Park on the back. We've given grid references within the book for each sight and listing.

🛳 Nearest riverboat or ferry stop
♿ Facilities for visitors with disabilities
🛈 Tourist information
❓ Other practical information

🎟 Admission charges:
   Expensive (over $12),
   Moderate ($5–$12) and
   Inexpensive (under $5)
▷ Further information

3

Introducing New York

"New York is an island off the coast of Europe." There's a lot of truth in this witticism, and it's no wonder this is the US city most overseas visitors choose first. The qualities that weld New Yorkers to the city also distinguish them from most Americans.

Residents of Manhattan, the most densely populated of New York City's boroughs, value directness, diversity and creativity; they live at a ridiculous pace; they work all hours (they have to, to pay the rent); they walk—fast—everywhere; they fail to keep their opinions to themselves; they are street smart; they are capital L Liberal. New York is a key Blue State, having voted Democrat in the last eight presidential elections, turning out in large numbers against native son Donald Trump. The city that actually lived through the horror of the 9/11 attack refuses to give in to fear; New Yorkers have all the chutzpah they ever did.

In New York, change is the only constant. The crime-ridden, graffiti-scarred mean streets of the late 20th century are all but a distant memory. In fact, these days New York is the safest large city in America (at least according to the NYPD). In stark contrast to the gritty days, you'll see strollers wherever you go, because there is a mini baby-boom in progress. Real-estate prices are in the realm of fiction, and a whole lot of regular folks have decamped for Brooklyn, while those who can't afford Brooklyn have gone to Queens. These days parts of Harlem are glamorous and beautiful; the Bronx is next. Staten Island, the fifth borough, which most visitors know only for its ferry, is the final frontier.

For many, Manhattan will always be the center of the universe. It's where deals are done, stars are born, legends—and fortunes—are made. Nowhere else in America offers such diversity in fashion, food, design, theater and the arts. The constant stimulation is addictive, and simply being here is worth a thousand inconveniences. You can take in only so much of the big picture in one visit. So do as New Yorkers do—find a corner of the city and make it your own.

FACTS AND FIGURES

- Visitors in 2018: 65.2 million (the ninth straight year that numbers have gone up)
- Dollars spent by visitors in 2016: $43 billion
- Hotel rooms by end of 2018: 115,530
- Population in 2017: 8.6 million
- Licensed yellow cabs: 13,587
- Feature films shot in New York: 28 movies, 18 TV series being filmed in 2018

REAL ESTATE

New York is in the midst of a building boom, with luxury skyscrapers that are among the tallest—and most expensive—in the world. This has put the squeeze on some middle-class New Yorkers. Still, many residents view their homes as not just their castles, but as their portfolio, their retirement plan and their chief financial burden.

BROOKLYN

Once a separate city, the vast borough of Brooklyn across the East River has experienced a migration of disaffected Manhattanites that has changed its character forever. Previously, Brooklyn wasn't fashionable; now it's a destination for excellent restaurants, good music venues, avant garde theater and great parties in those oh-so-desirable brownstones.

ONE WORLD TRADE CENTER

Nicknamed the Freedom Tower, the new tower in the World Trade Center (▷ 62–63) is officially called One World Trade Center (1WTC). It stands 1,776ft (541m) high—symbolic of the date of US independence—making it the tallest building in America. The stunning observatory opened to the public in spring 2015.

Focus On Architecture

New York is constantly changing, and nowhere is this more apparent than in its architecture. Skyscrapers symbolize the city, but it has many other gems, from ornate art deco office lobbies to the classical columns, carvings and statuary of its Beaux Arts public buildings.

Skyscrapers Past

Although Chicago erected the first skyscraper in 1885, New York embraced the high-rise building style so grandly that it has become the hallmark of the city's skyline. Among the earliest still standing is the 1899 Park Row Building, topped by its distinctive Beaux Arts domes, which at 391ft (119m) held the title of "world's tallest building" for nine years. Other notable early skyscrapers include the 1902 Flatiron Building by Daniel Burnham (▷ 68); the 700ft (213m) Metropolitan Life Insurance Tower (1909), modeled after St. Mark's Campanile in Venice; and the neo-Gothic Woolworth Building (1913), at 792ft (241m) the world's tallest until 1930.

In Lower Manhattan, skyscrapers grew so thick and fast that the streets of the Financial District started to turn into dark canyons. Zoning laws were passed in 1916, requiring builders to taper the upper stories with "set-backs" to allow light to reach ground level.

By 1930, the race for the top had become a battle of egos, as 40 Wall Street was trumped by the spire of the Chrysler Building (▷ 67), only to lose its title the following year to the Empire State Building (▷ 28–29). It remained the world's tallest building until the World Trade Center towers went up in 1972.

…and Present

From the 1950s onward, art deco elegance gave way to the glass "curtain wall" buildings of the International and Postmodern styles, so prominent in Midtown. The 21st century has

Clockwise from top left: Norman Foster's Hearst Tower; the triangular Flatiron Building; 19th-century Gramercy Park Historic District; interior of the US Custom House,

seen the addition of such new landmarks to the city skyline as Norman Foster's Hearst Tower (2006). One World Trade Center (▷ 5), completed in 2013, once again made the city home to the tallest building in the US. The 96-story 432 Park Avenue, completed in 2015, is the tallest apartment block in the world.

Civic and Residential Architecture
But there's so much more to New York's architecture than these high-rise wonders. Outstanding among its civic buildings are several Beaux Arts beauties, including the US Custom House (1907; ▷ 73), the New York Public Library (1911; ▷ 48–49) and Grand Central Terminal (1913; ▷ 34–35). SoHo Cast Iron Historic District (▷ 52–53) is lined with elaborate Italianate facades.

Residential architecture is also fascinating in this commercial city, from the brick tenements of the Lower East Side, with their zigzagging fire escapes, to the fine brownstone town houses, with their high stoops and elaborate doorways lining the leafy streets of Greenwich Village or Brooklyn Heights, to flamboyant luxury apartment buildings, like the Ansonia on Broadway and the Dakota overlooking Central Park on the Upper West Side.

Early Relics
Sadly, little remains in Manhattan from the city's earliest days. Seek out the colonial-era St. Paul's Chapel (▷ 72), the Federal-style warehouses of Schermerhorn Row at South Street Seaport (▷ 72), The Row, a line of Greek Revival houses on Washington Square (▷ 73), or the 19th-century houses surrounding Gramercy Park, once home to the likes of John Steinbeck (No. 38) and Joseph Pulitzer (No. 17). These survivors are gems in a city that is always tearing down the old to make room for the new.

one of New York's finest Beaux Arts buildings; The Row, Washington Square North; the spire of the Chrysler Building; the Woolworth Building's neo-Gothic facade

Top Tips For...

These great suggestions will help you tailor your ideal visit to New York, no matter how you choose to spend your time.

Star Chefs
Jean-Georges Vongerichten's restaurant (▷ 146) is the flagship of his ever-growing worldwide empire.
Daniel Boulud at **Café Boulud** will wow you (▷ 143). Save room for the desserts.
At **Eleven Madison Park** (▷ 144–145) chef Daniel Humm is a master of reinvention, with the most complex tasting menus in the city.
For superb fish, few match Eric Ripert at **Le Bernardin** (▷ 142).

Being On Trend
Trot over to **Jeffrey New York** (▷ 122) to refresh your wardrobe, or, for vintage, **Resurrection** (▷ 124–125).
Get a taste of the LES (Lower East Side) music vibe at the **Parkside Lounge** (▷ 135).
Have a late supper at gastropub **The Spotted Pig** (▷ 149).
Check out the latest art show at the **New Museum** (▷ 70) or go gallery hopping in **Chelsea** (▷ 66–67).

Partying till Dawn
On Friday and Saturday dance the night away to live Latin grooves at **SOB's** (▷ 137).
Go with the groove at the late-night jazz series at the **Blue Note** (▷ 132) from 12.30am on Friday and Saturday.
Ward off a hangover with a hearty breakfast or some Ukrainian soul food at cozy **Veselka** (▷ 149), open 24 hours.

Big and Beautiful Views
Harbor rooms at the **Ritz-Carlton Battery Park** (▷ 159) include a telescope.
Take in the lake view from Central Park's **Loeb Boathouse** (▷ 147).

Clockwise from top left: Vintage style for sale; view from the Top of the Rock at the Rockefeller Center; tiger enclosure at the Bronx Zoo; head to the Blue Note for

Top of the Rock (▷ 51), at the Rockefeller Center, rivals the **Empire State Building** (▷ 28–29) for views, but the **One World Observatory** (▷ 63) is the city's highest—you can see 50 miles (80km) on a clear day.

Bringing the Kids
You can never go wrong with a good zoo. **Bronx Zoo** (▷ 74) is vast; the one in **Central Park** (▷ 18–19) won't take all day. Take them to **Serendipity 3** (▷ 147) for frozen hot chocolate.
Get tickets for a family-friendly show at **The New Victory Theater** (▷ 135).
You could spend days exploring the **American Museum of Natural History** (▷ 14–15), from its dinosaur halls and Hall of Gems to the Space Theater.

Classic NYC
See the ceiling covered in toy trucks at the '21' Club (▷ 142).
Bergdorf's, Saks and **Bloomingdale's** are classic department stores with different personalities (▷ 120, 125).
The stunning **Chrysler Building** (▷ 67) is New York's favorite skyscraper and an art deco masterpiece.
Walk across the **Brooklyn Bridge** (▷ 66).

Sporting Pursuits
If you are here during baseball season (April to September), **Yankee Stadium** (▷ 75) is a must. Or catch the Mets at **Citi Field**.
Madison Square Garden (▷ 134) has it all: basketball (the Knicks), boxing, tennis, track and field, hockey, dog shows and more.
There's a game of something in progress in **Central Park** (▷ 18–19) all summer long. If it's winter, you can go skating at the **Wollman Rink**.
Brooklyn's **Barclays Center** is home to basketball and hockey (620 Atlantic Avenue).

late-night jazz; the pedestrian walkway, Brooklyn Bridge; Madison Square Garden; the New Museum; Café Boulud, bastion of fine cuisine

Timeline

Pre-1600 Native American groups populate New York area.

1609 Henry Hudson sails up the Hudson River seeking the Northwest Passage.

1625 "Nieuw Amsterdam" is founded by the Dutch West India Company on the tip of Manhattan Island. The following year the colony's leader purchases the island from the Native Americans for 60 guilders in trade goods.

THE FIGHT FOR INDEPENDENCE

In 1664, Wall Street's wall failed to deter the British, who invaded Manhattan Island and named it New York. The first rumblings of Revolution came in 1765, when Stamp Act protesters rallied in Bowling Green Park. In 1770, the Sons of Liberty fought the British at the Battle of Golden Hill, and in 1776, the American Revolutionary War began and the British chose New York as their headquarters. The Declaration of Independence was read at City Hall Park in July 1776 and the Treaty of Paris ended the war in 1783.

1664 In a bloodless coup, the British take over and rename the island New York.

1776 American Revolutionary War begins.

1785 New York becomes the capital of the United States (until 1790).

1789 George Washington is sworn in as first US president at Federal Hall.

1827 Slavery in New York is abolished.

1845 Start of the first great wave of immigrants after the Irish Potato Famine.

1863 Civil War Draft Riots divide the city.

1868 The city's first "El" (elevated train) opens.

1886 The Statue of Liberty is officially unveiled.

Inauguration of George Washington on the balcony of Federal Hall in 1789

Immigrants arriving in New York Harbor, 1892

1892 Ellis Island immigration center opens.

1904 The first subway opens.

1929 The Great Depression follows the Wall Street Crash.

1933 Prohibition ends after 14 years. Fiorello LaGuardia becomes mayor.

1954 Ellis Island is closed down.

1964 Race riots erupt in Harlem and Brooklyn.

1975 A federal loan saves New York City from bankruptcy.

1990 David Dinkins, New York's first black mayor, takes office.

2001 Terrorists fly two hijacked planes into the World Trade Center, killing nearly 3,000 people.

2011 The National September 11 Memorial opens at the World Trade Center Site.

2013 The new tower at One World Trade Center becomes the tallest skyscraper in America.

2017 More than 400,000 people jam the streets as part of a nation-wide Women's March in January.

2019 The Shed, the city's newest performing arts venue, opens as part of Hudson Yards, a massive new business and cultural center.

TENEMENT LIFE

As you make your first explorations in New York, consider how it was for the early immigrants, especially those who were herded through Ellis Island, then crammed into Lower East Side tenements. By the end of the 19th century, the immigrant neighborhoods were dominated by Italians and Eastern European Jews and had become the most densely populated place on earth. Many of these immigrants became garment workers in the ornate cast-iron buildings of SoHo, though many also sewed clothes at their overcrowded homes. Find out more at the Tenement Museum (▷ 72).

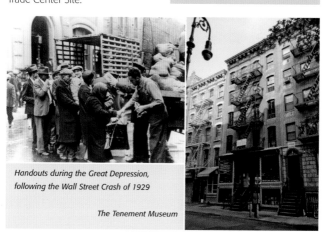

Handouts during the Great Depression, following the Wall Street Crash of 1929

The Tenement Museum

Top 25

This section contains the must-see Top 25 sights and experiences in New York. They are listed alphabetically, and numbered so you can locate them on the inside front cover.

1 American Museum of Natural History

HIGHLIGHTS

- Blue whale
- Titanosaur
- Cape York meteorite
- Dinosaur halls
- Journey to the Stars
- Star of India
- Animal dioramas
- Dinosaur embryo
- IMAX theater shows

TIP

● You can observe the entire life cycle of tropical butterflies from October to June at the Butterfly Conservatory.

Of the 36 million items owned by the American Museum of Natural History—the largest such institution in the world—only a small fraction is on show. Don't miss the renowned dinosaur halls and stunning animal dioramas in native habitats.

Star attractions The original museum building opened in 1877 and, as it grew, its facade sported pink brownstone and granite towers, turrets and a grand Beaux Arts entrance on Central Park West. This opens into a soaring rotunda containing the museum's beloved Barosaurus, and visitors soon encounter the museum's prized Titanosaur cast (so enormous that its head extends into the hallway). The museum is best known for its splendid dinosaur halls, where real fossil specimens (rather

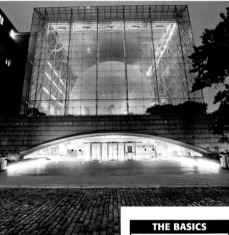

Left: the magnificent rotunda of the American Museum of Natural History is dominated by the skeleton of a Barosaurus; below: the stunning Rose Center for Earth and Space, adjoining the museum, includes the Hayden Planetarium, where space shows take place

than models) of an Apatosaurus and the first Tyrannosaurus rex ever exhibited are displayed. Another highlight is the enormous model of a blue whale looming over the Hall of Ocean Life. Equally impressive are the *tableaux morts* of animals from around the world, which are set in life-like scenes.

Gems and more The 563-carat Star of India sapphire is part of the Morgan Memorial Hall of Gems, which contains merely a fraction of the museum's precious stones. There's far too much to see in one day, with four city blocks and the entire evolution of life on Earth covered. In the adjoining Rose Center for Earth and Space, a giant sphere contains the Big Bang Theater and the Hayden Planetarium, where thrilling space shows are projected on the dome.

THE BASICS

amnh.org

✚ C6

✉ Central Park West/ 79th Street

☎ 212/769-5100

🕐 Daily 10–5.45

🍽 Various

🚇 B, C 81st Street– Museum of Natural History

🚌 M7, M10, M11, M79, M86

♿ Good

💲 Expensive

❓ 1-hour tours from 10.15 until 3.15. Call 212/769-5200 for advance reservations for special exhibits and events, including occasional sleepovers (some for children, others for adults only)

HIGHLIGHTS

- Williamsburg
- Brooklyn Heights Promenade
- Bandshell concerts
- The Brooklyn Academy of Music (BAM)
- Brooklyn Museum of Art

TIP

- Brooklyn Academy (BAM.org) and St. Ann's Warehouse (stannsware house.org) in Brooklyn offer some of New York's best avant garde theater.

Brooklyn has it all—one of the largest art museums in the US and some of New York's best restaurants; beaches and a park; a zoo, aquarium and children's museum; stylish neighborhoods and avant-garde arts.

Big, bigger, biggest If Brooklyn were still a separate city, it would be the fourth largest in the US. Home to more than 2.6 million people, it is the most populous of New York's boroughs, with Russian, Middle Eastern, Italian, West Indian, Hasidic Jewish and Chinese neighborhoods. The Brooklyn Museum, one of the largest in the US, has collections ranging from pre-Columbian art to 58 Rodin sculptures, plus what many feel are the best Egyptian rooms outside Egypt and the British Museum. Its newly renovated, and now even larger, "Art of

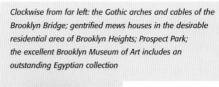

Clockwise from far left: the Gothic arches and cables of the Brooklyn Bridge; gentrified mews houses in the desirable residential area of Brooklyn Heights; Prospect Park; the excellent Brooklyn Museum of Art includes an outstanding Egyptian collection

THE BASICS

Brooklyn Heights
✚ H22
🚇 2, 3 Clark Street
Brooklyn Museum
brooklynmuseum.org
✚ See map ▷ 110
✉ 200 Eastern Parkway
☎ 718/638-5000
🕐 Wed, Fri–Sun 11–6, Thu 11–10
🚇 2, 3 Eastern Parkway–Brooklyn Museum
💲 Expensive
Prospect Park
prospectpark.org
✚ See map ▷ 110
☎ 718/965-8951
🚇 2, 3 Grand Army Plaza Station; F 15th Street–Prospect Park
Williamsburg
✚ See map ▷ 111
Brooklyn Flea's Smorgasburg
smorgasburg.com
✉ Saturday: East River State Park, 90 Kent Avenue. Sunday: Prospect Park–Breeze Hill. Summer months only; check website for details
🚇 L train closed until summer 2020. Use alternate bus (mta.info) or ferry (ferry.nyc). (Sun) Prospect Park Subway
💲 Inexpensive

Korea" Gallery has a renowned collection of Korean art. Steps from the museum's grand entrance is the Botanic Garden. Then, farther south, wander in Prospect Park, where summertime events and the zoo are highlights.

The bridge and beyond Brooklyn Bridge Park is an 85-acre (34ha) greenway reclaimed from derelict piers along the Brooklyn Heights waterfront, with jogging paths, water sports and outdoor festivals. From Brooklyn Heights you can climb stairs to the Brooklyn Bridge pedestrian crossing or visit the Promenade for its view of Manhattan. Williamsburg is among the trendiest spots, known for its restaurants, clubs, artisanal foods and crafts and, in warm weather, the renowned Brooklyn Flea's Smorgasburg artisanal food market in an outdoor setting.

HIGHLIGHTS

- Delacorte Theater, Shakespeare in the Park
- Summer stage concerts
- Conservatory Water
- Bethesda Fountain
- Wollman Rink in winter
- Heckscher Playground
- Swedish Cottage Marionette Theatre
- Walking in the Ramble

TIPS

- Don't walk alone in isolated areas at night.
- Watch out for bicycles on the roads.

The park is the escape valve for the city. Without it New York would overheat—especially during the summer, when the temperature rises. Bikers, runners, dog walkers and frisbee players convene here. It's a way of life.

The Greensward Plan In the mid-19th century, when few lived in Manhattan north of 42nd Street, *New York Evening Post* editor William Cullen Bryant campaigned until the city invested $5 million in 843 acres (340ha) of undeveloped land. Responsible for clearing the land was journalist Frederick Law Olmsted, who, with English architect Calvert Vaux, also won the competition to design the park with his "Greensward Plan." Five million cubic tons of dirt were cleared to create this green space.

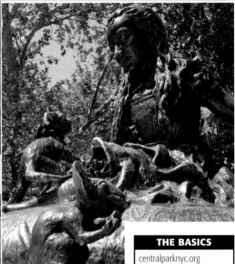

Clockwise from left: the Pond, at the south end of Central Park; a bronze statue depicting characters in Lewis Carroll's Alice in Wonderland, *just north of the Conservatory Water; Sheep Meadow, a great place to throw frisbees; the tribute to John Lennon in Strawberry Fields*

Fun and games Start at the Dairy Visitor Center and pick up a map and events list. These show the layout of the park and tell you about the Wildlife Conservation Center (Zoo), the Carousel, the playgrounds, rinks, fountains, statues and Strawberry Fields, where John Lennon is commemorated close to the Dakota Building, where he lived and was shot. But the busy life of the park is not recorded on maps: making music on the Mall; sunbathing in Sheep Meadow; hanging out at the Heckscher Playground and Great Lawn softball leagues; doing the loop road by bike; sailing toy boats on the Conservatory Water; bird-watching in the Ramble; jogging around the Reservoir; rowing on the Lake beneath the lovely Bow Bridge; fishing at Harlem Meer; or bouldering on the outcrops of Manhattan schist (rock).

THE BASICS

centralparknyc.org
➕ D2–D9 (see reverse of sheet map)
☎ 212/310-6600
🅾 Dairy Visitor Center, 65th Street, daily 10–5; 3 other kiosks throughout the park
🍽 Restaurants, kiosks
🚇 A, B, C, D, 1 59th Street–Columbus Circle; N, Q, R, W 57th Street–7th Avenue; N, R, W 5th Avenue–59th Street; F 57th Street; B, D 72nd Street
🚌 M1, M2, M3, M4, M5, M10. Crosstown M66, M72, M79, M86
♿ Moderate
🆓 Free

★ 4 Chinatown

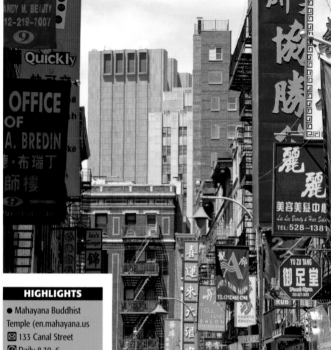

- Mahayana Buddhist Temple (en.mahayana.us
✉ 133 Canal Street
⏰ Daily 8.30–6
💰 Donation)
- Museum of Chinese in America (▷ 70)
- New Kam Man (200 Canal Street, ▷ 124)
- Doyers Street
- Columbus Park
(✉ Bayard/Baxter streets)

TIP

- Visit Columbus Park, where you can see everything from fortune tellers to tai chi to Chinese singers and instrumentalists, who perform near the pavilion on weekends.

New York's Chinatown has swallowed nearly all of Little Italy and has spread over a great deal of the Lower East Side. Wander here and become immersed by the sights and sounds of a busy Asian community.

Going west Chinese people first came to New York in the late 19th century, fleeing persecution on the west coast. But, by 1880, some 10,000 men—mostly Cantonese railroad workers—had settled among the Irish and Italians of the old Five Points area. The Chinese Exclusion Act (1883) kept the community small until immigration restrictions were lifted in 1965. While the first arrivals were mostly Cantonese speakers, most of today's immigrants are Fujianese. New York has two more Chinatowns: in Flushing (Queens) and Eighth

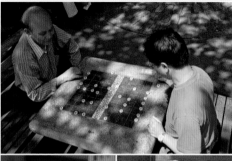

Clockwise from left: a colorful and vibrant area, Manhattan's Chinatown is a long-established Asian enclave and one of the largest Chinatowns outside Asia; a quiet spot for a Chinese board game; a statue of Confucius; snakeskins for sale at a Chinese herbalist

Avenue, Brooklyn, with thousands of residents. Manhattan's, though, is the second-largest in the western hemisphere.

A closed world Although Chinatown is welcoming to visitors, you might never penetrate its culture. Many of its inhabitants never learn English and never leave its environs. Many work in the neighborhood's restaurants, which range from hole-in-the-wall dumpling joints to those serving old-fashioned Cantonese fare that recollect an earlier era. Catch a glimpse of this vibrant culture at the Mahayana Buddhist Temple, with its 16ft (4.9m) Buddha; in the markets that line Canal and Grand streets; or at the Museum of Chinese in America (▷ 70), which tells the story of New York's Chinese community from its birth to the present day.

THE BASICS

explorechinatown.com
✚ F19–F20
✉ Roughly delineated by Worth Street/East Broadway, the Bowery, Grand Street, Centre Street
🍴 Numerous (some close around 10pm)
🚇 6, J, N, Q, R, Z Canal Street; B, D Grand Street
🚌 M22, M103
♿ Poor
❓ Visitors' Kiosk at Canal and Baxter streets, daily 10–6

---

5 Cooper Hewitt Smithsonian Design Museum

- Original 1903 detailing
- HD touch-screen tables
- Immersion Room
- Process Lab
- Design Triennial
- Summer concerts
- Textile collection

TIP

● The renovated garden is free to the public and is open Mon–Fri 8–6, Sat 10–9, Sun 10–6. The café is also free to visit.

America's national design museum is a marvelous showcase of everything from cutting-edge work by up-and-coming artists to classic examples of fine furnishings and accessories. All of it is housed in one of New York's most stunning mansions.

Carnegie, Cooper and Hewitt The mansion that contains this superb collection belonged to industrialist Andrew Carnegie, who, in 1903, had asked architects Babb, Cook & Willard for "the most modest, plainest and most roomy house in New York City." This he did not receive (aside from the roominess), since this little chateau was built with modern conveniences galore—air-conditioning and elevators—and a big gated garden. The entire neighborhood came to be known as

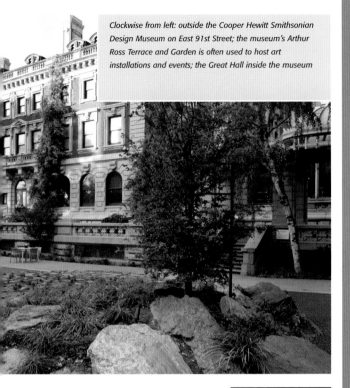

Clockwise from left: outside the Cooper Hewitt Smithsonian Design Museum on East 91st Street; the museum's Arthur Ross Terrace and Garden is often used to host art installations and events; the Great Hall inside the museum

Carnegie Hill. Andrew's wife, Louise, lived here until her death in 1946. Twenty years later, the collection of the Hewitt sisters (decorative arts, ceramics, textiles and more), which had been previously exhibited at the Cooper Union (▷ 24), became a part of the Smithsonian and moved into the mansion.

State of the art The museum's recent revamp was designed to make its exhibitions more interactive. In the Immersion Room, you can project textile patterns onto blank walls and then create your own. In the Process Lab, you can make your own protoype or see a 3D printer in action. However, these state-of-the-art exhibits have not displaced the Hewitt sisters' core collection and Carnegie's home is still shown to good effect.

THE BASICS

cooperhewitt.org
➕ E4
✉ 2 E 91st Street
☎ 212/849-8400
🕐 Sun–Fri 10–6, Sat 10–9
🍴 Café
🚇 4, 5, 6 86th Street
🚌 M1, M2, M3, M4
♿ Good
💰 Expensive (by donation Sat 6–9pm)
❓ Free tours daily

HIGHLIGHTS
● Merchant's House Museum
● Exploring St. Mark's Place
● Diverse array of foods

TIP
● The Strand (▷ 125) on Broadway has 18 miles (29km) of shelves packed with new and used titles. In an area that was once lined with second-hand bookshops, the Strand is one of the few remaining places to find obscure titles.

Once an immigrant neighborhood—and then the rundown bohemia celebrated in the musical *Rent*—the East Village is now prime real estate. Nearby NoHo is quieter and full of historic streets and sites.

Early days What was once Dutch Governor Peter Stuyvesant's farm, or bowery, later became a mostly German enclave. Jews, Poles and Ukrainians followed. Meanwhile, streets such as Bond and Lafayette, in what is today called NoHo (North of Houston), were home to New York's mercantile elite, including John Jacob Astor, the country's richest man.

Historic sites Cooper Union, founded by industrialist Peter Cooper and built in 1859, was the spot where Abraham Lincoln gave his

Clockwise from far left: Cooper Union, an East Village landmark; trading on the area's literary associations; the neighborhood's Ukrainian heritage is celebrated at the Ukrainian Museum; architectural detail inside Grace Church; an East Village mural

landmark "Right Makes Might" anti-slavery speech. The city's second-oldest church, St. Mark's Church-in-the-Bowery, boasts Peter Stuyvesant's grave. On Broadway, Grace Church was the debut of architect James Renwick, who went on to build St. Patrick's Cathedral (▷ 71). The Ukrainian Museum, in the heart of the immigrant neighborhood, features textiles and beautifully decorated Easter eggs. In NoHo, the Merchant's House Museum is an intact early 19th-century home lived in by the same family for nearly a century.

St. Mark's Place The main thoroughfare of the East Village is St. Mark's. In the 1960s, counter-culture exploded along this street, which included Andy Warhol's Electric Circus. Today it is a mix of shops, restaurants and tattoo parlors.

THE BASICS

➕ F16; east of Broadway and south of 14th Street
🚇 F, M Lower East Side—2nd Avenue; 6 Astor Place

Ukrainian Museum
ukrainianmuseum.org
➕ F17
✉ 222 E 6th Street/2nd–3rd avenues
☎ 212/228-0110
🕐 Wed–Sun 11.30–5
♿ Good 💲 Moderate

Merchant's House Museum
merchantshouse.org
➕ E17
✉ 29 E 4th Street/Lafayette–Bowery
☎ 212/777-1089
🕐 Thu 12–8, Fri–Mon 12–5; tours at 2pm
♿ Poor 💲 Expensive

HIGHLIGHTS

● Wall of Honor
● Peopling of America galleries
● The American Flag of Faces™

TIP

● To avoid lines and wait times, try to be on the first ferry to Ellis Island at 8.30 (which also serves the Statue of Liberty). The lines to board ferries grow during the day, especially in summer. The last ferry departs at 3.30pm.

Visiting Ellis Island, the gateway to America for millions of immigrants from 1892 to1954, is a poignant reminder of the obstacles so many people had to overcome to reach this country.

Half of all America It was the poor immigrants who docked at Ellis Island, since travelers in first-class passage were given permission to disembark straight into Manhattan. Young Annie Moore, aged 15 and the first immigrant to land at Ellis Island, arrived in 1892. She was followed by some 16 million immigrants over the next 60 years, including such future success stories as Irving Berlin and Frank Capra. Unsurprisingly, around one-third of the current population of the United States can trace their roots to an Ellis Island immigrant.

Clockwise from far left: exhibition documenting the arrival of early immigrants to New York; statue of Annie Moore, the first immigrant to arrive at Ellis Island; inside the Great Hall; view of Ellis Island from the ferry; the view of Lower Manhattan from Ellis Island; an immigrant's records

Island of Hope, Island of Tears The exhibition in the main building conveys the indignities, frustrations and fears of the immigrants. Choose a ranger-guided tour or the free, 45-minute audio tour which accompanies you around the route that new arrivals took, from the Baggage Room, where people had to abandon all they owned, then onward to the Registry Room and through the inspection chambers, where the medical, mental and political status of each immigrant was ascertained. In the museum, the American Family Immigration History Center® gives access to passenger ship records of millions of immigrants (for a fee). The Peopling of America galleries tell of the hardships and struggles of immigrants in the years before and after the island's processing station.

THE BASICS

nps.gov/elis

➕ See map ▷ 110

✉ Ellis Island

☎ 212/363-3200

🕐 Daily 9.30–5; extended hours in summer

🍴 Café

🚇 4, 5 Bowling Green, 1 South Ferry, then take ferry

🚌 M5, M20, M15 South Ferry, then take ferry

⛴ Ferry departs Battery Park South Ferry every 30 min. Ferry information tel 877/523-9849, statuecruises.com

♿ Good

💲 Museum free; ferry expensive

❓ Audio tours

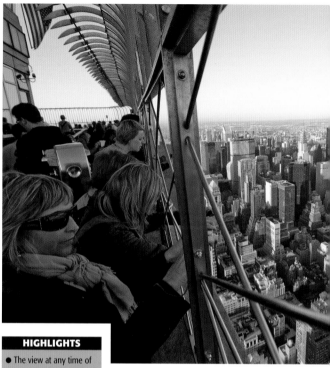

HIGHLIGHTS

● The view at any time of day or night
● The view up from 34th Street
● Observatory audio tour
● Marble art deco lobby

TIPS

● Save time (though not the security check) by printing out advance tickets from the website. Express Passes for an extra fee bypass lines.
● The colored lights at the summit were introduced in 1976 and are changed to mark different events.

Though it lost its crown as the world's tallest building more than four decades ago, the Empire State Building remains New York's most famous skyscraper. Known around the world from movies such as *King Kong*, *An Affair to Remember* and *Sleepless in Seattle*, the 86th-floor Observatory is worth the long lines.

King for 40 years This is the very definition of "skyscraper," and it was the highest in America until the late, lamented World Trade Center was built in the 1970s. Now it has once again been overtaken as the tallest building in New York, this time by One World Trade Center (▷ 63). Construction began in 1930, not long after the great Wall Street Crash. By the time it was topped out in 1931—construction went at

Left: head to the Observatory on the 86th floor for panoramic views of New York; below: there are good views of the Empire State Building itself from 34th Street

the superfast rate of four stories a week—few could afford to rent space, and they called it the "Empty State Building." Only the popularity of its observatories kept the wolves from the door. These views still attract up to four million visitors each year. The open-air 86th floor Observatory is a highlight.

The facts It is 1,454ft (443m) high, with 103 floors. The frame contains 60,000 tons of steel, 10 million bricks line the building, and there are 6,500 windows. The speediest elevator climbs about 1,000ft (300m) per minute. The fastest runners in the annual Empire State Run-Up climb the 1,860 steps (not open to the public) to the 102nd floor in just over nine minutes. The observation deck on the 102nd floor requires a separate ticket and an additional fee.

THE BASICS

esbnyc.com

➕ E13

✉ 350 5th Avenue/ W 34th Street

☎ 212/736-3100

🕐 Daily 8am–2am; last admission 1.15am; Sunrise Experience on selected days (100 tickets per day)

🍽 Restaurants

🚇 B, D, F, N, Q, R, W 34th Street–Herald Square

🚌 M1, M2, M3, M4, M5

🚆 PATH 34th Street–Avenue of the Americas

♿ Good

💲 Expensive

TOP 25

HIGHLIGHTS

- Shopping!
- Empire State Building
- Rockefeller Center
- The Met
- The Guggenheim
- Cooper Hewitt

TIP

- Try to see a parade—St. Patrick's Day Parade, the biggest, is on March 17.

Fifth Avenue is still the grand old dame of New York shopping, its Midtown section lined with prestigious stores. There's a lot more to see along this 6-mile (10km) thoroughfare though—famous museums, historic mansions and glorious Central Park.

Tradition and invention Fifth Avenue runs all the way from Washington Square Park up past Central Park and houses some of the most pricey and notable real estate in New York. Walk along the avenue and you'll pass the Flatiron Building (▷ 68), the Empire State Building (▷ 28–29), the New York Public Library (▷ 48–49), Rockefeller Center (▷ 50–51), St. Patrick's Cathedral (▷ 71), the Frick Collection (▷ 32–33), the Metropolitan Museum of Art (▷ 44–45), the Guggenheim

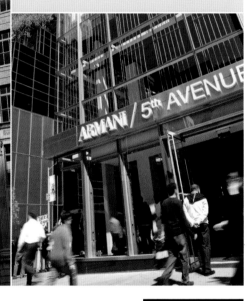

Clockwise from far left: for most visitors Fifth Avenue is synonymous with shopping; Saks Fifth Avenue, one of New York's most prestigious department stores; designer brands abound; the Cooper Hewitt Smithsonian Design Museum

(▷ 38–39) and the Cooper Hewitt Smithsonian Design Museum (▷ 22–23), just a few of the buildings that represent the development of Fifth Avenue.

Shop, shop, shop Stores along Fifth are generally high end, but window shopping is encouraged. Start with the jewelry emporia of Tiffany & Co. (57th Street) and Cartier (No. 653), the 24-hour Apple Store (▷ 119) or the department stores. Saks Fifth Avenue (▷ 125) has been here since 1922. Bergdorf Goodman (▷ 120) is at 58th Street, and Armani and Gucci are at 56th, along with Abercrombie & Fitch. If you plan to shop till you drop, two excellent hotels stand opposite each other on Fifth Avenue and 55th Street: the Peninsula New York and the St. Regis (▷ 159).

THE BASICS

🔯 E16–E7

✉ From Washington Square to the Harlem River

🚇 4, 5, 6 (various stops), N, R, W 5th Avenue–59th Street; E, M 5th Avenue–53rd Street

🚌 M1, M2, M3, M4

HIGHLIGHTS

● *St. Jerome*, El Greco (c.1590–1600)
● *Sir Thomas More*, Holbein (1527)
● *Officer and the Laughing Girl*, Vermeer (c.1657)
● *The Polish Rider*, Rembrandt (c.1655)
● *The Progress of Love*, Fragonard (1771–72)
● *Philip IV of Spain*, Velázquez (1644)

To step inside Henry Clay Frick's magnificent Beaux Arts mansion on Fifth Avenue is half the reason for coming here. Henry Frick bequeathed his riches to the nation as a memorial to himself—that's the kind of guy he was.

The man and the mansion Henry Clay Frick (1849–1919) was chairman of the Carnegie Steel Corp. He was a ruthless strike-breaker and one of the nastiest industrialists of his day. Instead of receiving any comeuppance (though there were assassination attempts), he got to commission Carrère and Hastings to build him one of the last great Beaux Arts mansions on Fifth Avenue and filled it with an exquisite collection of 14th- to 19th-century paintings, porcelain, furniture and bronzes.

Clockwise from left: the Garden Court is at the heart of the collection; the Fragonard Room displays works by Holbein, El Greco, Titian and Bellini; the Fifth Avenue Garden

What Frick bought Some of the 16 galleries are arranged around a particular work or artist, notably the Boucher Room, east of the entrance, and the Fragonard Room, with the *Progress of Love* series. There are British (Constable, Gainsborough, Whistler, Turner), Dutch (Vermeer, Rembrandt, Van Eyck, Hals), Italian (Titian, Bellini, Veronese) and Spanish (El Greco, Goya, Velázquez) masters. Alongside the paintings are Limoges enamel and Chinese porcelain, Persian carpets and Marie Antoinette's furniture. You can admire a Louis XVI chair before strolling through the central glass-roofed courtyard. The Fifth Avenue Garden is also a delight. An anticipated renovation of The Frick Collection is scheduled to begin in 2020. Check the website before you visit in case there are revised opening times.

THE BASICS

frick.org

E7

✉ 1 E 70th Street

☎ 212/288-0700

🕐 Tue–Sat 10–6, Sun 11–5. First Fri of the month 6–9pm (free)

🚇 6 68th Street–Hunter College

🚌 M1, M2, M3, M4

♿ Good

💲 Expensive (pay what you wish Wed 2–6pm)

❓ Audio tours; for concerts, lectures and docent talks see calendar

HIGHLIGHTS

- Main concourse ceiling
- Oyster Bar
- Chandeliers
- Whispering Gallery
- The clock
- The 75ft (23m) arched windows
- Grand Staircase
- The Dining Concourse (▷ 145)
- Great Northern Food Hall

TIP

- After admiring the building, visit the many boutiques, gourmet market and annex of the New York Transit Museum.

Officially called Grand Central Terminal because the tracks all terminate here, this Beaux Arts masterpiece is not only an architectural marvel but also one of the biggest stations in the world.

Heart of the nation "Grand Central Station!" bellowed (erroneously) the 1937 opening of the eponymous NBC radio drama; "Beneath the glitter and swank of Park Avenue… Crossroads of a million private lives!…Heart of the nation's greatest city…" And so it is, and has been since 1871, when the first, undersize version of the station was opened by Commodore Cornelius Vanderbilt, who had bought up all the city's railroads. See him in bronze below Jules Alexis Coutan's allegorical statuary on the main facade (south, 42nd Street). The current

Clockwise from far left: the concourse of Grand Central Terminal; statuary by Jules Alexis Coutan on the main facade; Grand Central subway station; the Great Northern Food Hall; the four-faced clock; enjoy a platter of oysters in the famous Oyster Bar

THE BASICS

grandcentralterminal.com

➕ E11

✉ E 42nd Street/Park Avenue

☎ 212/340-2583

🕐 Daily 5.30am–2am

🍴 Restaurant, café/bar, snack bars

🚇 4, 5, 6, 7, S Grand Central–42nd Street

🚌 M1, M2, M3, M4, M42, M101, M102, M103 Grand Central

🚆 Metro North, Grand Central

♿ Good

🆓 Free

❓ Both self-guided audio tours (moderate; daily 9–6) and the guided Municipal Art Society tours (expensive; daily 12.30pm) leave from the GCT Tour windows on the main concourse

building dates from 1913 and is another Beaux Arts glory, its design modeled partly on the Paris Opéra by the architectural firm Warren and Wetmore.

Look within Inside, the main concourse soars 12 stories high, with gleaming gold chandeliers and grand marble staircases at either end. Be careful what you say here—the acoustics are amazing. Look up at the ceiling for the stunning sight of 2,500 "stars" in an azure sky, with zodiac signs by French artist Paul Helleu. The fame of the brass clock with its four opalescent glass faces atop the information booth is out of proportion to its size. Below ground is a warren of 32 miles (52km) of tracks, tunnels and chambers; in one the famed Oyster Bar (▷ 148) resides.

HIGHLIGHTS

- Charming boutiques
- Washington Square Park
- NYC's narrowest house
(75½ Bedford Street)
- Christopher Park
- Halloween parade
- Jefferson Market Library
- Italian restaurants on
Bleecker Street
- MacDougal Street

TIP

- Free Tours by Foot is one
of several groups offering
guided tours; many self-
guided tours are available
online.

The Village (never just "Greenwich") has
long been a bohemian mecca, and its
picturesque neighborhoods, lined with
trees and brownstones, form a romantic
image of Manhattan.

Artists, writers, musicians First settled by the
Dutch as Noortwijck, the Village became a
refuge in the 18th and early 19th centuries for
wealthy New Yorkers escaping epidemics in the
city. When the elite moved on, the bohemian
invasion began. Edgar Allan Poe moved to West
Third Street in 1845. Fellow literary habitués
included Mark Twain, O. Henry, Walt Whitman,
F. Scott Fitzgerald and Eugene O'Neill. After
World War II, artists Jackson Pollock, Mark
Rothko and Willem de Kooning also lived here.
Bob Dylan made his name in Village music

Clockwise from far left: bars and restaurants abound in the Village; detail of the Gay Liberation Monument in Christopher Park; Bleecker Street has many restaurants; Christopher Street has great shops; getting around in the Village; desirable St. Luke's Place

clubs in the 1960s, while the Blue Note (▷ 132) and Village Vanguard clubs remain hotbeds of jazz today.

Freedom parades When police raided the Stonewall Inn on June 28, 1969, and arrested gay men for illegally buying drinks, they set off the Stonewall Riots—the birth of the Gay Rights movement. The Inn is on Christopher Street, which became the center of New York's gay community. Statues of gay and lesbian couples stand in tiny Christopher Park. The Washington Memorial Arch (▷ 73) towers over Washington Square Park, a lively hangout for university students. As you explore, look out for the ornate Jefferson Market Library (6th Avenue and W 10th Street), the quaint Cherry Lane Theatre on Commerce Street, and tiny Minetta Lane.

THE BASICS

✚ C17–D17
✉ East–west from Broadway to Hudson Street; north–south from 14th Street to Houston Street
🍴 Numerous
🚇 A, B, C, D, E, F 4th Street–Washington Square; 1 Christopher Street–Sheridan Square
🚌 M5
🚈 PATH Christopher Street
♿ Poor

HIGHLIGHTS

● The building
● *L'Hermitage à Pontoise*, Pissarro (1867)
● *Paris Through the Window*, Chagall (1913)
● *Woman Ironing*, Picasso (1904)
● *Nude*, Modigliani (1917)
● Kandinskys
● Klees
● Légers
● The store

TIP

● Museum admission is pay-what-you-wish on Saturdays 5.45–7.45, but get there early as lines can be long.

Now considered one of his masterpieces, Frank Lloyd Wright's spiral-shaped museum building was originally derided by critics, who compared it to a jello mold.

Museum of architecture This is the great architect's only major New York building. It was commissioned by Solomon R. Guggenheim at the urging of his friend and taste tutor Baroness Hilla von Rebay though, unfortunately, the wealthy metal-mining magnate died 10 years before it was completed in 1959. The giant white nautilus is certainly arresting, but it's the magnificent interior that captures the imagination the most. Take the elevator to the top level and snake your way down the museum's spiral ramp to experience the full effects of the building's design. You can study

*Left: the spiral walkway inside the Guggenheim Museum;
below: the Guggenheim's curvy exterior*

the exhibits (albeit in reverse order), look over the parapet to the lobby below, and finish up where you began.

Museum of art There are some 6,000 pieces in the foundation's possession. Solomon and his wife Irene Rothschild abandoned collecting old masters when Hilla von Rebay introduced them to Léger, Kandinsky, Chagall, Mondrian, Moholy-Nagy and Gleizes, and they became hooked on the moderns. See early Picassos in the small rotunda and the tower extension. For Impressionists and Postimpressionists, look for the Thannhauser Collection, always on display—unlike the rotated Guggenheim holdings, which are shown in themed exhibitions. The museum still acquires works, including pieces by Matthew Barney and Agathe Snow.

THE BASICS

guggenheim.org

🔒 E5

✉ 1071 5th Avenue/
89th Street

☎ 212/423-3500

🕐 Sun–Wed, Fri 10–5.45,
Sat 10–7.45

🍴 Café

🚇 4, 5, 6 86th Street

🚌 M1, M2, M3, M4

♿ Good

💲 Expensive

❓ Lecture program;
audio tours

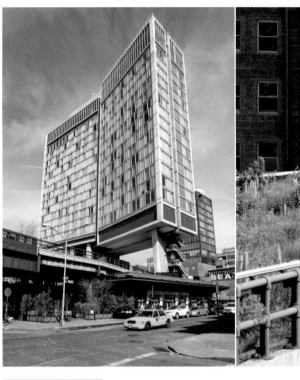

HIGHLIGHTS

- The Whitney Museum
- Site-specific art installations
- Northern spur preserve
- 10th Avenue Square
- High Line Plinth

TIP

- Because the park keeps entirely to the original rail line, narrow sections can be crowded. Come early before the day heats up or enjoy a leisurely stroll just before sunset.

Today this beautiful elevated park attracts more annual visitors than the Statue of Liberty. Yet just a decade ago, the High Line was a weed-choked, abandoned rail line snaking through the industrial waterfront.

Train tracks Manhattan in the 19th century was the largest port in America, with many commercial piers lining the Hudson River. To move the huge amount of goods, Tenth Avenue was overlaid with railroad tracks so dangerous that the street was nicknamed Death Avenue. In the early 1930s, the trains were moved to a second-story elevated track running through many of the factories and warehouses, including the giant Nabisco headquarters (birthplace of the Oreo cookie) that is now Chelsea Market (▷ 121).

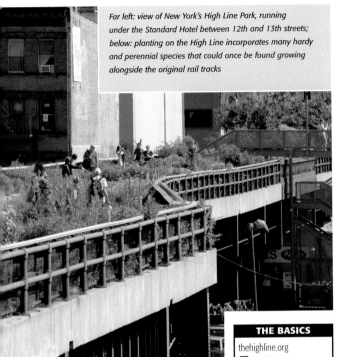

Far left: view of New York's High Line Park, running under the Standard Hotel between 12th and 13th streets; below: planting on the High Line incorporates many hardy and perennial species that could once be found growing alongside the original rail tracks

Friends of the High Line After the freight line folded, the abandoned sections of track became overgrown. In 1999, Friends of the High Line formed to advocate turning this wilderness into an amenity. A park was opened and now stretches 1.45 miles (2.3km) from Gansevoort Street to West 34th Street. Its popularity has transformed the surrounding neighborhood, drawing new luxury condos, hotels (such as the Standard) and restaurants. Where the tracks cross 10th Avenue at 17th Street, seating allows visitors to gaze uptown; a few steps south, an overgrown spur track recalls what the High Line looked like before renovation. In summer, the park hosts temporary exhibitions, plus the High Line Plinth at the Spur, with contemporary art. The park's southern end joins the home of the Whitney Museum of American Art (▷ 60–61).

THE BASICS

thehighline.org
✚ A13, B13–16
✉ Gansevoort Street to W 34th Street between 10th and 12th avenues (staircases or elevators up to the park located every 2–3 blocks)
☎ 212/500-6035
🕐 Daily Jun–Sep 7am–11pm; Apr–May, Oct–Nov 7am–10pm; Dec–Mar 7–7
🍴 Seasonal
🚇 A, C, E 14th Street; L 8th Avenue; 7 34th Street–Hudson Yards
🚌 M11, M12, M14, M23, M34
👆 Free
♿ Good

⭐ 15 Lincoln Center

HIGHLIGHTS

● Chandeliers in the Met foyer and auditorium
● Reflecting Pool with Henry Moore's *Reclining Figure* (1965)
● Lincoln Center Out-of-Doors Festival in summer
● New York City Ballet's *Nutcracker* in December
● Chagall murals in the foyer of the Met
● Free concerts at the David Rubenstein Atrium
● New York Film Festival
● The Revson Fountain in the Central Plaza
● Jazz at Lincoln Center
● Annual *Messiah* singalong

TIP

● Dance under the stars at the Midsummer Night's Swing, and enjoy summer events in adjacent Damrosch Park.

Strolling across the Central Plaza to the fantastically lit 10-story colonnade of the Metropolitan Opera House on a deep winter's night is one of the most glamorous things you can do in this city, and you don't need tickets to come and look.

West Side Story The Rockefeller-funded arts center was envisaged in the late 1950s and finished in 1969, after 7,000 families and 800 businesses had been pushed aside by city planner Robert Moses. The opening scene of *West Side Story* was filmed here after the demolition began.

All the arts The 16-acre (6ha) site includes several of New York's top arts venues, all designed by different architects in the same

Clockwise from left: the Revson Fountain, between the David H. Koch Theater (left) and the Metropolitan Opera House (right); the David Rubenstein Atrium is a great place to meet up with friends; aerial view of the Lincoln Center at night

white travertine. The Metropolitan Opera House is the glamor queen, with her vast Marc Chagall murals, red carpet, fabulous sweeping staircase and sparkling chandeliers that thrillingly rise to the gold-leaf ceiling before performances. You can take a fascinating backstage tour. David Geffen Hall is home to America's oldest orchestra, the NY Philharmonic, while the Juilliard School of Music supplies the ensemble with fresh talent. The David H. Koch Theater, housing the New York City Ballet, faces David Geffen Hall across the Plaza. The Frederick P. Rose Hall is the centerpiece of Jazz at Lincoln Center in the Time Warner Center down the street. Lincoln Center Theater, with three stages, the intimate Alice Tully Concert Hall and two movie theaters—Walter Reade and Elinor Bunin—complete the pack.

THE BASICS

lincolncenter.org

✚ B8

✉ 64th Street at Columbus Avenue

☎ Met Opera 212/362-6000, David Geffen Hall 212/875-5030, Jazz 212/258-9800

🕐 Inquire for performance times

🍴 Restaurants, cafés, bars

🚇 1 66th Street–Lincoln Center

🚌 M5, M7, M10, M11, M66, M104

♿ Good

🎫 Center admission free

❓ Tours daily from David Rubenstein Atrium, tel 212/875-5350

HIGHLIGHTS

● Temple of Dendur
(15BC)
● Period rooms, American
Wing
● 19th- and early 20th-
century art galleries
● Decorative arts from the
Far East
● Greco-Roman galleries

TIP

● On Friday and Saturday
evenings, when the
museum stays open late,
enjoy a cocktail and live
music on the mezzanine.

The largest art museum in the western
hemisphere has something for everyone,
from ancient artifacts to arms and armor,
cutting-edge fashion and some of the most
famous paintings in the world.

Art history 101 The Met's collection is
renowned for its stunning breadth and depth.
In fact, the museum is so huge that visitors are
advised either to do a whirlwind tour (with or
without a museum guide) or to choose one
period or area to explore in depth, whether
that's ancient Greece, Africa or the summer
rooftop installations.

Buildings upon buildings The Met is housed
in three locations: the main museum on Fifth
Avenue, The Cloisters in Upper Manhattan

Clockwise from left: the Met's European Sculpture Court; Wheat Field with Cypresses, Vincent van Gogh (1889), in the European Paintings and Sculpture Room; the Beaux Arts facade of the museum

(European medieval art ▷ 74) and the Met Breuer (with modern and contemporary art ▷ 68–69), a few minutes away on Madison Avenue. There are treasures to be discovered inside the main headquarters, including the Egyptian temple of Dendur, the Astor Court (a Ming dynasty courtyard) in the Chinese galleries, a Frank Lloyd Wright living room in the American wing, and the beautifully decorated Damascus room in the Islamic collection.

Special exhibitions and more The museum hosts homegrown and traveling exhibitions (included in the admission fee) along with concerts, lectures, gallery talks and site-specific music and dance events (for an extra charge). Check the museum's website in advance for these, as many special events sell out quickly.

THE BASICS

metmuseum.org
➕ D5–6
✉ 1000 5th Avenue/82nd Street
☎ 212/535-7710
🕐 Sun–Thu 10–5.30, Fri–Sat 10–9
🍴 Café, restaurant, bar
🚇 4, 5, 6 86th Street
🚌 M1, M2, M3, M4
♿ Good
💲 Expensive
❓ Free guided tours leave from the information desk in the main lobby every 15 minutes, 10.15–4

HIGHLIGHTS

● *Hope*, Klimt (1907–08)
● *Dance*, Matisse (1909)
● *Les Demoiselles d'Avignon*, Picasso (1907)
● *Starry Night*, Van Gogh (1889)
● *Gas*, Hopper (1940)
● *One: Number 31*, Pollock (1950)
● *Flag*, Jasper Johns (1954–55)
● Sculpture Garden
● Free garden concerts on Thursdays in summer

Yoshio Taniguchi's MoMA expansion in 2004 doubled the museum's gallery space; now the museum is growing again, providing even more room to showcase its unmatched collection of everything from Postimpressionist paintings to film.

Postimpressionists to graffiti artists Founded on the 1931 bequest of Lillie P. Bliss, which comprised 235 works of art, MoMA's collections now amount to about 150,000 pieces. These include household objects, photography, graphic design, conceptual art, industrial design and media. The collection starts in the late 19th century, with the Postimpressionists and later Fauvists. Among the 20th-century movements represented in the museum are Cubism, Futurism, Expressionism, Surrealism, Abstract

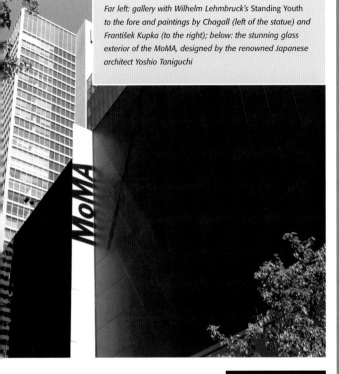

Far left: gallery with Wilhelm Lehmbruck's Standing Youth to the fore and paintings by Chagall (left of the statue) and František Kupka (to the right); below: the stunning glass exterior of the MoMA, designed by the renowned Japanese architect Yoshio Taniguchi

Expressionism, Pop (Oldenburg, Dine, Rauschenberg and Warhol) and the "Graffiti" work of Keith Haring and Jean-Michel Basquiat.

Even more modern A sunlit atrium, 110ft (34m) high, affords a view of the Abby Aldrich Rockefeller Sculpture Garden, a museum favorite containing such works as Picasso's *She-Goat* (1950) and Barnett Newman's *Broken Obelisk* (1963–69). The Sculpture Garden is open daily at 9.30, except in bad weather, and is free of charge until 10.15am. Taniguchi's building makes much use of glass, granite, aluminum and light, and individual galleries have been designed specifically for the media they house. Audio tours are available for download to your smartphone. There is a second location (MoMA PS1) in Queens.

THE BASICS

moma.org
🔳 D10
✉ 11 W 53rd Street/ 5th–6th avenues
☎ 212/708-9400
🕐 Sat–Thu 10.30–5.30, Fri 10.30–8
🍴 Restaurant
Ⓜ E, M 5th Avenue–53rd Street; B, D, F 47th–50th streets–Rockefeller Center
🚌 M1–M5, M7
♿ Good
💲 Expensive (includes special exhibitions and films); free Fri 4–8

18 New York Public Library

HIGHLIGHTS

- Patience and Fortitude
- Rose Reading Room
- Thomas Jefferson's handwritten Declaration of Independence
- Astor Hall
- American Jewish Oral History Collection
- Gottesman Hall ceiling

TIP

- It's worth taking one of the free one-hour tours (Mon–Sat 11, 2; Sun 2). Meet at the reception desk in Astor Hall.

The New York Public Library's Central Research Building is a great white, hushed palace, beautiful to behold even if you have no time to open any of its books. It is a US National Historic Landmark.

The building Along with the US Custom House (▷ 73) and Grand Central (▷ 34–35), this masterpiece by Carrère and Hastings is ranked as one of the best Beaux Arts buildings in New York and is a highlight of what was known as the City Beautiful era. In 2011 the library was rechristened the Stephen A. Schwarzman Building, after the Wall Street financier who donated $100 million toward its ongoing renovation. A pair of lions, named Patience and Fortitude by Mayor LaGuardia during the Depression, flank the stair that leads into the

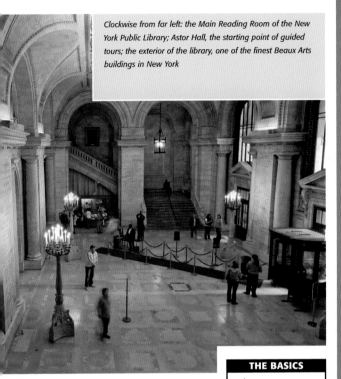

Clockwise from far left: the Main Reading Room of the New York Public Library; Astor Hall, the starting point of guided tours; the exterior of the library, one of the finest Beaux Arts buildings in New York

white marble Astor Hall. Inside, see temporary exhibitions in the Gottesman Hall, and look skyward: the carved oak ceiling is sublime. Priceless items from the library's collection, such as the first Gutenberg Bible brought to the New World, line the balcony corridor or are displayed in upstairs rooms. Don't miss the stunning two-block-long reading rooms, or the Richard Haas murals of NYC publishing houses in the De Witt Wallace Periodical Room.

The books The library owns more than 18 million books, most of which are kept in the 92 branches. The 92 miles (148km) of holdings are solely for research. Books kept on the premises are sent to the reading room by dumbwaiter; for material kept offsite, researchers must make an appointment.

THE BASICS

nypl.org
🚹 E12
✉ 476 5th Avenue/42nd Street
☎ 917/275-6975
🕐 Tue, Wed 10–8, Thu–Sat 10–6, Sun 1–5
🍴 Kiosks outside (summer)
🚇 4, 5, 6, S Grand Central–42nd Street; 7 5th Avenue
🚌 M1, M2, M3, M4, M5, M7, M42
🚆 Metro North, Grand Central
♿ Good
💲 Free

HIGHLIGHTS

- Top of the Rock Observation Deck
- 30 Rock's lobbies and the Lee Lawrie friezes
- NBC Studio tour
- Skating in winter
- Radio City Music Hall
- *Prometheus* (1934)
- *Atlas* (5th Avenue, 50th–51st streets)

TIP

- There's a vast array of shops, casual restaurants and more in a basement arcade below the center. There's a great vantage point for watching winter skaters down there, too.

This complex of art deco buildings provides many of those "this really is New York" moments, especially at Christmas when you can watch ice-skaters ringed by the flags of the UN and gaze up at the massive tree.

Prometheus is here The 19-building Rockefeller Center has been called the greatest urban complex of the 20th century. John D. Rockefeller Jr.'s grand real estate scheme provided work for 40,000 people during the Depression. Its centerpiece is the elongated ziggurat at 30 Rockefeller Plaza (officially now the Comcast Building, formerly the GE Building), adorned with Lee Lawrie's glass-and-limestone frieze, lobby murals by José Maria Sert and various other artworks. Rest for a while on a Channel Gardens bench and gaze on the

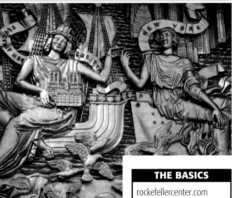

From far left: Radio City Music Hall forms part of Rockefeller Center; Paul Manship's bronze Prometheus *(1934) on the Lower Plaza;* Friendship Between America and France *(1934), a gilded bronze by Alfred Janniot above the Fifth Avenue entrance*

Lower Plaza, the ice rink and Paul Manship's gilded bronze *Prometheus* (1934).

Top of the Rock The three-tiered observation deck on the 70th floor of 30 Rock affords stunning panoramic views over Manhattan and the only public overview of Central Park. The mezzanine museum tells the history of the complex before high-speed elevators whisk you to the 67th to 70th-floor viewing platforms.

NBC and Rockettes This is also the home of NBC Studios. Tours are led daily, or try for standby tickets to *Saturday Night Live* or one of the late-night talk shows filmed here. At Christmas time (and now in summer), the Rockettes hold court at Radio City Music Hall (▷ 136), the grandest theater in town.

THE BASICS

rockefellercenter.com
➕ D10–11, E10–11
✉ 5th–6th avenues/ 48th–51st streets
☎ 212/588-8601
🕐 Various
🍴 Many restaurants, cafés
🚇 B, D, F, M 47th–50th streets–Rockefeller Center
🚌 M1, M2, M3, M4, M5, M7, M50
♿ Moderate
🎫 Free
❓ Radio City tours, tel 212/465-6741; NBC Studio tours, tel 212/664-3700; Rockefeller Center tours, tel 212/698-2000

Top of the Rock
topoftherocknyc.com
☎ 212/698-2000
🕐 Daily 8am–12.30am (last elevator 11.55pm)
🎫 Expensive

HIGHLIGHTS

- Shopping
- King and Queen of Greene Street
- Little Singer Building
- Haughwout Building

TIP

- Stop at Dean & DeLuca (Broadway and Prince) for a coffee and pastry, a hot sandwich or to browse its delectable gourmet fare, including its cheese and dessert counters.

In the last 150 years, SoHo has come full circle. New York's smartest shopping district around the time of the Civil War, the area fell on hard times by World War II. Now, its landmark cast-iron buildings teem with fashionable shops again.

Cast in iron An acronym for "South of Houston," SoHo stretches for several delightful blocks between Houston and Canal streets, bordered by Lafayette Street on the east and Sixth Avenue to the west. Around 500 of its 19th-century industrial buildings have been preserved in the SoHo Cast Iron Historic District. Inexpensive, strong and easy to mold, cast iron made it possible to erect ornate buildings in Italianate and other elaborate styles quickly and cheaply. Some of the finest examples

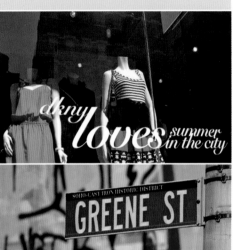

Clockwise from far left: the Little Singer Building in the SoHo Cast Iron Historic District; sculpture inspired by the well-known 1932 photograph of New York ironworkers eating lunch while sitting on a girder; fashion stores; Greene Street is a great place to stroll; art galleries abound

dkny *loves* summer in the city

SOHO-CAST IRON HISTORIC DISTRICT
GREENE ST

are the King (No. 72) and Queen (No. 28) of Greene Street, the Little Singer Building (561 Broadway) and the Haughwout Building (488 Broadway), which had the first Otis steam passenger elevator. Old-fashioned lampposts further enhance SoHo's charm.

Art and fashion By the 1960s and 1970s, many of SoHo's commercial buildings were abandoned. Then, artists moved in, art galleries followed, and SoHo became the most fashionable quarter in town. Rising prices forced many artists and galleries to Chelsea and beyond, but fashionistas quickly filled the empty and spacious showrooms. Everything from Prada's flagship store to branches of Bloomingdale's and Britain's Topshop, and designer boutiques, make this a shopper's heaven.

THE BASICS

🞢 E18–19
✉ Houston–Canal streets, Lafayette Street–6th Avenue
🍽 Numerous
🚇 R, W Prince Street; C, E, 6 Spring Street
🚌 M5, M21
♿ Moderate

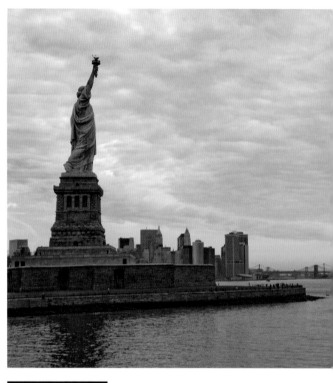

HIGHLIGHTS

● View from the crown
● Statue of Liberty Museum, including the original torch
● Fort Wood, the star-shaped pedestal base

TIP

● Visits to the crown must be reserved well in advance (sometimes 3–4 months) on tel 201/604-2800 or online at statuecruises.com. There are no same-day crown tickets available.

Liberty Enlightening the World (as she's formally known), famous symbol of the American dream of freedom, takes your breath away, however many times you've seen her image.

How she grew In the late 1860s, sculptor Frédéric-Auguste Bartholdi dreamed of placing a monument to freedom in a prominent location. His dream merged with the French historian Edouard-René de Laboulaye's idea of presenting the American people with a statue that celebrated freedom and the two nations' friendship. Part of the idea was to shame the repressive French government but, apparently, New Yorkers took their freedom for granted. It was only after Joseph Pulitzer promised to print the name of every donor in his newspaper, the

From left: Liberty Island, a beacon of hope since 1886; Liberty's seven-pointed crown; the symbol of American liberty raises her torch to the world

New York World, that citizens coughed up the funds to build the pedestal. Liberty was unveiled by President Grover Cleveland on October 28, 1886.

Mother of exiles Beneath her 25ft-long (8m) feet, she tramples the shackles of tyranny, and her seven-pointed crown beams liberty to the seven continents and the seven seas. Gustave Eiffel designed the 1,700-bar iron and steel structure that supports her. She weighs 225 tons, is 151ft (46m) tall, and is covered in 300 copper plates. The tablet she holds reads: July IV MDCCLXXVI—the date of the Declaration of Independence. The torch tip towers 305ft (93m) above sea level. In the museum in the statue's base you can read Emma Lazarus's stirring poem, *The New Colossus*.

THE BASICS

nps.gov/stli

➕ See map ▷ 110

✉ Liberty Island

☎ 212/363-3200

🕐 Daily 8.30–5 (last ferry departs 3.30); extended hours in peak season. A limited number of daily tickets to tour the pedestal/ museum may be reserved in advance from the ferry office, by phone or online

🍴 Café

🚇 4, 5 Bowling Green, 1 South Ferry, then take ferry

🚌 M5, M15, M20 South Ferry, then take ferry

⛴ Departs Battery Park

☎ 877/523-9849; statuecruises.com

♿ Poor

💲 Free; ferry expensive

HIGHLIGHTS

- Neon lights at night
- Broadway Plaza
- 42nd Street
- ABC's *Good Morning* studio: 44th/Broadway
- New Year's Eve ball drop

TIP

- The TKTS booth at Duffy Square, 47th Street/Broadway, discounts same-day theater tickets and is open daily 3–8 for evening shows, Wed, Thu and Sat 10–2 for matinees, Sun 11–3 for matinees, 3–7 for evening shows. Other locations: Lincoln Center and South Street Seaport.

"The Crossroads of the World," one-time symbol of Manhattan glitz and glamor, is bright, bold and exciting—there is always something going on here. Beneath the dazzling neon signs, big-name stores and entertainment venues do a brisk trade.

Longacre Square The junction of Broadway and Seventh Avenue was called Longacre Square until the Times Tower, the new home of the *New York Times*, was finished in 1904. Almost immediately, the relocation of the theater district, the opening of the first subway and the decision to site the New Year celebration here made it the symbolic center of Manhattan.

On Broadway The theaters moved into the area, and Broadway, the Great White Way,

Clockwise from far left: detail on the old Paramount Theater, a Times Square landmark; New Victory Theater, which specializes in family entertainment; bright lights, big city; New Year's Eve revelers; visitors flock to Times Square for shopping, family attractions and the full-on neon experience

became synonymous with big-time showbiz with its popular shows, particularly musicals. By 1914 there were some 43 theaters in the immediate vicinity of the square; after multiple closures, refurbishments and reopenings, there are 41 of them today.

Best of Times, worst of Times By the 1970s Times Square was decaying, many of the legitimate theaters having fallen on hard times and become porn theaters. But a massive clean-up effort in the 1990s brought about the area's rebirth. Today it's a tourist hot spot, with a raft of family attractions, megastores and restaurants beneath the glittering state-of-the-art illuminations. A large section of Times Square is now traffic-free, though the human traffic jams are bigger than ever.

THE BASICS

timessquarenyc.org

➕ D11

🚇 1, 2, 3, 7, N, Q, R, S Times Square–42nd Street

🚌 M5, M7, M20, M42, M104

❓ Visit the Tourist Information kiosk in Broadway Plaza for up-to-date happenings in and around the square

TKTS Booth: tdf.org/nyc/81/TKTS-Live provides real-time updates of what is on offer before you commit to standing in line

HIGHLIGHTS

- Trinity Church
- Federal Hall
- New York Stock Exchange
- The House of Morgan

TIP

- Weekend mornings are quietest in this part of town. To experience the hustle and bustle of Wall Street traders, come Mon–Fri around lunch.

Depending on your point of view, Wall Street is the blessing or blight of the world's economic fortunes. But either way, the historic buildings and urban buzz of this financial powerhouse are fascinating to see and experience.

The Buttonwood Agreement Wall Street, named for the Dutch colonial wall that once marked the city's northern boundary, is the epicenter of the financial district. It has been so since the late 18th century, when businessmen gathered here under a buttonwood tree to trade bonds, issued to finance debts incurred in the Revolutionary War. In 1792, 24 traders signed the Buttonwood Agreement, which created the New York Stock Exchange. Today the NYSE is the largest stock exchange in the

Clockwise from far left: the New York Stock Exchange; the soaring towers of Wall Street; Federal Hall, fronted by a bronze statue of George Washington and modeled on the Greek Parthenon; the beautifully decorated domed ceiling in the entrance of Federal Hall

world. The 1903 building, with its grand trading floor and facade of Corinthian columns, stands at the corner with Broad Street.

A million-dollar stroll At the west end of Wall Street stands Trinity Church (1846), the third on this site. The original, built in 1699, was the city's first church. Alexander Hamilton and other famous New Yorkers are buried in the church-yard. At the corner of Wall and Broad streets sits the House of Morgan, formerly owned by J.P. Morgan & Co, and once the most powerful financial institution in America (now housing apartments). On April 30, 1789, George Washington was sworn in as America's first president at Federal Hall, now a national memorial and museum. 40 Wall Street is also known as the Trump Building.

THE BASICS

downtownny.com
nps.gov/feha
moaf.org
trinitywallstreet.org

✚ E22

✉ NYSE, 18 Broad Street; Federal Hall, 26 Wall Street; Trinity Church, Broadway at Wall Street

☎ Federal Hall 212/825-6990; Trinity Church 212/602-0800

🕐 Federal Hall Mon–Fri 9–5; Trinity Church daily 7–6

🍴 Restaurants, pubs

🚇 2, 3, 4, 5 Wall Street; J, Z Broad Street

🚌 M5

🎟 Federal Hall free; Trinity Church free

❓ Tours: Download Trinity Church's guided tour app from its website

HIGHLIGHTS

● Whitney Biennial
● *Brooklyn Bridge*, Joseph Stella (1939)
● Hoppers
● O'Keeffes
● *Dempsey and Firpo*, George Bellows (1924)
● Nevelsons

TIP

● Make certain you enjoy the museum's outdoor spaces, with great views of the Hudson, the High Line and Midtown.

Gertrude Vanderbilt Whitney's world-class collection, a showcase of her work and that of her friends, was first shown in a modest Greenwich Village studio space in 1918. Today, the collection is housed in the stunning and innovative Renzo Piano-designed headquarters along the High Line.

No room at the Met Sculptor and patron of her contemporaries' work, Gertrude Vanderbilt Whitney offered her collection of 700 modern artworks to the Met in 1929, but the great institution turned up its nose. Whitney instead formalized her own museum space, first in the Village, and then on the Upper East Side. Renzo Piano's Meatpacking District building has greatly expanded the museum's footprint, allowing more room for shows. The Whitney's collection

Left: the museum's new home is a 21st-century architectural gem; below: the Whitney hosts a biennial exhibition of contemporary art

WHITNEY BIENNIAL

reads like a roll call of American 20th-century greats: Edward Hopper, Thomas Hart Benton, Willem de Kooning, Georgia O'Keeffe, Claes Oldenburg, Jasper Johns, George Bellows and Jackson Pollock are perhaps the best known.

Take your pick Exhibitions, drawn from the museum's permanent collection, often emphasize a single artist's work. At other times they prove more eclectic. The Whitney Biennial (in the spring of even-numbered years) presents the curator's vision—sometimes controversial—of the leading trends in American art during the past two years and often features the work of lesser-known artists. The famous showcase has boosted careers of artists such as Edward Hopper (who appeared in the inaugural exhibition in 1932), Sheila Hicks and Jenny Holzer.

THE BASICS

whitney.org
🚌 B16
✉ 99 Gansevoort Street/ Washington Street
☎ 212/570-3600
🕐 Sun–Mon, Wed–Thu 10.30–6, Fri–Sat 10.30–10
🍴 Restaurant, café
🚇 A, C, E 14th Street; L 8th Avenue
🚍 M14
♿ Good
💲 Expensive (under 18s free); donation Fri 7–10pm
❓ Free daily tours

HIGHLIGHTS

● Memorial waterfalls
● One World Observatory
● 9/11 Museum
● One World Trade Center
● Oculus Transportation Hub (the most expensive train station ever)

TIP

● While admission to the museum and to the observatory are expensive, it is free at all times to visit the memorial.

The twin towers of the World Trade Center, once the tallest buildings in the world, were a New York icon until they were destroyed by terrorists who crashed two hijacked planes into them on September 11, 2001. From the ashes, a moving memorial and a museum have risen that pay tribute to those who lost their lives in the tragedy.

The National September 11 Memorial and Museum An international contest was held to select a fitting memorial for the site. Architects Michael Arad and Peter Walker's design, entitled "Reflecting Absence," was chosen. It comprises two square waterfalls, situated over the footprint of the towers. The waterfalls cascade 30ft (9m) into pools that disappear into a center void. Bronze panels are inscribed with the

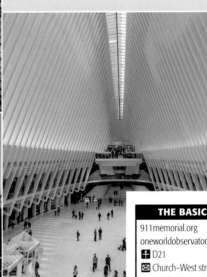

Clockwise from far left: waterfalls at the National September 11 Memorial; One World Observatory; the Oculus mezzanine, designed by Santiago Calatrava; the National September 11 Memorial at Ground Zero

names of almost 3,000 known victims of this and a bomb attack on the towers in 1993. A memorial park with more than 300 oak trees offers a peaceful space for contemplation. The underground museum provides a history of the site. New towers have transformed the area, along with Santiago Calatrava's futuristic Oculus, a combination transportation hub and lavish shopping center.

One World Observatory At the top of One World Trade Center (presently America's tallest building) is One World Observatory, with 360-degree views of Manhattan, Brooklyn, New York Harbor and beyond. "Sky Pods" (elevators) with stunning animations of Manhattan's 400-year development whisk visitors up to the 100th-story view in 60 seconds.

THE BASICS

911memorial.org
oneworldobservatory.com
✚ D21
✉ Church–West streets, Vesey–Liberty streets
☎ Memorial and museum: 212/266-5211; observatory: 844/696-1776
🕐 Memorial: daily 7.30am–9pm; museum: Sun–Thu 9–8 (last entry at 6), Fri–Sat 9–9 (last entry at 7); observatory: daily 9–8; longer in summer
🚇 E World Trade Center; 2, 3, 4, 5, A, C, J, Z Fulton Street
🚍 M5, M20, M22
♿ Good
💲 Memorial free; museum and observatory expensive; limited free tickets Tue 4–close

More to See

This section contains other great places to visit if you have more time. Some are in the heart of the city while others are a short journey away, found under Farther Afield. This chapter also has fantastic excursions that you should set aside a whole day to visit.

In the Heart of the City

AMERICAN FOLK ART MUSEUM

folkartmuseum.org

The outstanding collection of quilts is a highlight in this museum spanning the rich variety of folk art, from paintings and pottery to textiles and woodcarving; exhibits date from the 18th century to the present day. The museum's shop stocks a superb range of handcrafted items.

➕ C8 ✉ 2 Lincoln Square (Columbus Avenue between 65th and 66th streets) ☎ 212/595-9533 🕐 Tue–Thu, Sat 11.30–7, Fri 12–7.30, Sun 12–6 🚇 1 66th Street–Lincoln Center 🎟 Free

BATTERY PARK

thebattery.org

At the southernmost tip of Manhattan, with splendid views of New York Harbor, Battery Park was named for the cannon sited here to defend the fledgling city against British attack. Ferries to the Statue of Liberty and Ellis Island leave from Castle Clinton National Monument, a former fort. Among the many monuments in the park, look for the Immigrants (near Castle Clinton), a symbol of New York's enduring role as a city of emigrés.

➕ E23 ✉ Tip of Manhattan 🚇 1 South Ferry; 4, 5 Bowling Green

BROOKLYN BRIDGE

Completed in 1883, the Brooklyn Bridge was the first to link Manhattan and Brooklyn. With its twin Gothic towers and graceful ballet of cables, it is one of New York's finest landmarks. Stroll across the pedestrian walkway for views of the Manhattan skyline.

➕ G21 🚇 4, 5, 6 Brooklyn Bridge–City Hall

CHELSEA GALLERY DISTRICT

When real-estate prices in SoHo began to skyrocket in the 1990s, the downtown galleries moved to Chelsea. Today, there are over 100 galleries in the neighborhood, primarily located between 10th and 11th avenues. As most galleries are closed on both Sunday and Monday, art lovers should plan accordingly. Gallery

The American Folk Art Museum

Brooklyn Bridge

hopping, you can take in everything from established artists to Modernist masters to stars of the up-and-coming generation.
➕ B14 ✉ From 30th Street south to 17th Street, and 9th Avenue west to the Hudson River 🚇 1, 14th, 18th, 23rd, 28th streets–7th Avenue; C, E 14th, 23rd streets–8th Avenue

CHRYSLER BUILDING
The gleaming art deco spire of the Chrysler Building is an iconic symbol of New York. When completed in 1931, it held the title of "world's tallest building" until it was surpassed by the Empire State Building the same year. Every detail of the 77-story building evokes a 1929 Chrysler Plymouth. The winged steel gargoyles are modeled on its radiator caps; the building's stepped setbacks carry stylized hubcaps and the spire resembles a radiator grille. You can visit the lobby to see the art deco detailing in the red marble, granite and chrome interior, surmounted by the 97ft by 100ft (30m by 31m) mural depicting industrial

The Chrysler Building

scenes and celebrating "transportation." Don't miss the art deco marquetry on the elevator doors.
➕ F11 ✉ 405 Lexington Avenue/42nd Street 🕐 Mon–Fri office hours 🚇 4, 5, 6, 7, S Grand Central–42nd Street 🚌 M42, M101, M102, M103 🚆 Metro North, Grand Central ♿ Good 💲 Free

CITY HALL
nyc.gov/html/artcom
Built between 1803 and 1812 in Federal and French Renaissance styles, this is one of the nation's oldest city halls. The building and the rotunda, with its Corinthian columns and coffered dome, are designated landmarks. See the Governor's Room furniture and portrait collection on a guided tour.
➕ E21 ✉ Broadway/Murray Street ☎ 311 or 212/788-2656 🕐 Wed noon (register on the day 10–11.30 at the NYC tourism kiosk at the southern end of City Hall Park, east side of Broadway at Barclay Street) and Thu 10 (online reservations required) 🚇 2, 3 Park Place; 4, 5, 6 Brooklyn Bridge–City Hall; R City Hall 💲 Free

ELDRIDGE STREET SYNAGOGUE
eldridgestreet.org
Built in 1887, this synagogue is a symbol of the aspirations of Eastern European immigrants on the Lower East Side. Its 50ft (15m) vaulted ceiling, Moorish and Romanesque details and stained-glass windows make it one of the city's architectural gems. Exhibits and guided tours point out design features and tell the story of this diverse neighborhood.
➕ G19 ✉ 12 Eldridge Street ☎ 212/219-0302 🕐 Sun–Thu 10–5, Fri 10–3 🚇 F East Broadway; B, D Grand Street ♿ Good 💲 Expensive

FLATIRON BUILDING
This 1902 skyscraper, designed by Daniel Burnham, was named for its amazing and memorable shape. It is an isosceles triangle with a sharp angle pointing uptown.
⊕ E14 ✉ 175 5th Avenue/E 22nd–23rd streets 🚇 N, R 23rd Street

GULLIVER'S GATE
gulliversgate.com
From the Great Wall of China to the Egyptian pyramids to New York City, wonders of the world in miniature await at this attraction near Times Square, in a lavish display covering 50,000sq ft (4,645sq m).
⊕ D11 ✉ 216 W 44th Street ☎ 212/235-2016 🕐 Daily10–8 🚇 1, 2, 3, 7, N, Q, R, S Times Square 💰 Expensive

ITALIAN AMERICAN MUSEUM
italianamericanmuseum.org
In the heart of Little Italy, this small museum explores the history and heritage of America's Italian immigrants. Exhibits range from New York policeman Frank Serpico's guns to a collection of marionettes from the 1920s and 1930s.
⊕ F19 ✉ 155 Mulberry Street/Grand Street ☎ 212/965-9000 🕐 Fri–Sun 12–6 🚇 N, R Prince Street; F, V Broadway–Lafayette 💰 Donation

JEWISH MUSEUM
thejewishmuseum.org
The largest Jewish museum in the western hemisphere chronicles Jewish experiences worldwide. Artifacts in the permanent collection cover 4,000 years of Jewish history, while special exhibitions focus on Jewish art and culture.
⊕ E4 ✉ 1109 5th Avenue/92nd Street ☎ 212/423-3200 🕐 Sat–Tue 11–5.45, Thu 11–8, Fri 11–4, closing earlier Nov–Feb 🍴 Café 🚇 4, 5, 6 86th Street 💰 Expensive; free Sat and Thu eve

MET BREUER
metmuseum.org
When the Whitney Museum decamped for Chelsea from its Marcel Breuer-designed headquarters uptown, the Metropolitan Museum scooped up the property to showcase modern and contemporary artwork and performances. Using the Met's own collection as

New York's Jewish Museum chronicles the history of Jews worldwide

a starting point, the new satellite campus (free with paid admission to the nearby Fifth Avenue building) brings together artwork from around the world, and places newer pieces in the context of work stretching back to the Renaissance. Download *Soundwalk 9:09* by John Luther Adams to listen to as you walk between the two buildings.

➕ E7 ✉ 945 Madison Avenue/E 75th Street ☎ 212/731-1675 🕐 Tue–Thu, Sun 10–5.30, Fri–Sat 10–9 🍴 Café and restaurant 🚇 6 77th Street 💲 Expensive

MORGAN LIBRARY & MUSEUM

themorgan.org

This collection of literary works, rare musical manuscripts and artworks was amassed by financier J.P. Morgan, whose palatial library alone is worth the visit. Highlights include a copy of the Gutenberg Bible, music scores by Beethoven, Mozart and Puccini, etchings by Raphael and Michelangelo and manuscripts by Dickens and Twain.

➕ E12 ✉ 225 Madison Avenue/E 36th Street ☎ 212/685-0008 🕐 Tue–Thu

10.30–5, Fri 10.30–9, Sat 10–6, Sun 11–6 🚇 6 33rd Street; 4, 5, 6, 7 Grand Central 💲 Expensive

EL MUSEO DEL BARRIO

elmuseo.org

This museum dedicated to Latin American and Caribbean art contains over 8,000 items, from pre-Columbian artifacts to modern paintings and photographs.

➕ E2 ✉ 1230 5th Avenue/104th Street ☎ 212/831-7272 🕐 Wed–Sat 11–6, Sun 12–5 🚇 6 103rd Street 💲 Moderate

MUSEUM OF ARTS AND DESIGN

madmuseum.org

Affectionately known as MAD, the museum showcases crafts, art and design through an impressive collection, special exhibitions and public programs, while the monthly Studio Sundays allow families to join creative activities.

➕ C9 ✉ 2 Columbus Circle ☎ 212/299-2777 🕐 Tue, Wed, Fri–Sun 10–6, Thu 10–9 🍴 Restaurant 🚇 1, A, B, C, D 59th Street–Columbus Circle 💲 Expensive (by donation Thu 6–9pm)

Museum of Arts and Design

MUSEUM OF CHINESE IN AMERICA

mocanyc.org

The permanent collection tells the story of Chinese immigration across the USA. Temporary exhibits examine aspects of the contemporary Chinese-American experience.

➕ F19 ✉ 215 Centre Street/Grand Street ☎ 212/619-4785 ⏰ Tue–Wed, Fri–Sun 11–6, Thu 11–9 🚇 6, J, N, Q, R, Z Canal Street 💵 Moderate

MUSEUM OF THE CITY OF NEW YORK

mcny.org

Tells the story of the city since 1624. It has an outstanding collection of photographs, as well as toys, furniture and decorative arts.

➕ E2 ✉ 1220 5th Avenue/103rd Street ☎ 212/534-1672 ⏰ Daily 10–6 🚇 6 103rd Street 💵 Expensive ❓ Walking tours offered

NATIONAL GEOGRAPHIC ENCOUNTER: OCEAN ODYSSEY

natgeoencounter.com

This new virtual-reality experience at Times Square uses technology

Neue Galerie

to take visitors on an underwater journey across the Pacific Ocean to see stunning sea creatures, including whales and sharks.

➕ D11 ✉ 226 West 44th Street/7th and 8th avenues ☎ 646/308-1337 ⏰ Sun–Thu 10–9, Fri–Sat 9am–10pm 🚇 Times Square 💵 Expensive

NEUE GALERIE

neuegalerie.org

Dedicated to early 20th-century German and Austrian art and design, the highlight is Gustav Klimt's portrait *Adele Bloch-Bauer I* (1907). European decorative arts and the Bauhaus are also well represented in the collection, with contributions from the likes of Marcel Breuer, Theodor Bogler and Walter Gropius.

➕ E5 ✉ 1048 5th Avenue/86th Street ☎ 212/994-9493 ⏰ Thu–Mon 11–6 🍴 Café 🚇 4, 5, 6 86th Street 💵 Expensive

NEW MUSEUM

newmuseum.org

The dynamic building resembling giant white boxes stacked askew is a fitting home for this cutting-edge museum of contemporary art. The seventh-floor balcony affords panoramic views.

➕ F18 ✉ 235 Bowery/Prince Street ☎ 212/219-1222 ⏰ Tue–Sun 11–6, Thu until 9pm (pay what you wish) 🍴 Café 🚇 N, R Prince Street 💵 Expensive

NEW-YORK HISTORICAL SOCIETY

nyhistory.org

With 1.6 million objects dating from the Dutch Colonial era to the tragic events of 9/11, the society's exhibitions reveal key chapters in New York's past. Admission includes the film *New York Story*, an immersive, 18-minute narrative of the city's growth from Dutch trading port to world economic powerhouse. Many key objects are on view just inside the main entrance, including fragments from America's first capitol building and the shackles of a child who was held in slavery.

➕ C6 ✉ Central Park West/77th Street ☎ 212/873-3400 🕓 Tue–Thu and Sat 10–6, Fri 10–8, Sun 11–5 🚇 B, C 81st Street 💲 Expensive

RUBIN MUSEUM OF ART

rubinmuseum.org

A superb collection of art from Tibet and the Himalayan region. It comprises religious art and cultural artifacts, including scroll paintings, sculptures, ritual objects, textiles and prints. There is also a rich program of cultural events, such as music, meditation and movies.

➕ D15 ✉ 150 W 17th Street/7th Avenue ☎ 212/620-5000 🕓 Mon, Thu 11–5, Wed 11–9, Fri 11–10, Sat–Sun 11–6 🍴 Café 🚇 1 18th Street–7th Avenue 💲 Expensive, free Fri 6–10

ST. PATRICK'S CATHEDRAL

saintpatrickscathedral.org

With its ornate spires soaring 330ft (100m) above Fifth Avenue, James Renwick's cathedral, built in 1858–79, seats 2,200 people. The St. Michael and St. Louis altar was designed by Tiffany & Co., while the rose window is one of stained-glass artist Charles J. Connick's finest creations.

➕ E10 ✉ 5th Avenue between E 50th and E 51st streets ☎ 212/753-2261 🕓 Daily 6.30am–8.45pm; services at various times 🚇 6 51st Street; E, M 5th Avenue–53rd Street 💲 Free

ST. PATRICK'S OLD CATHEDRAL

oldcathedral.org

New York's first Roman Catholic cathedral opened in 1815, when the area was settled by Irish immigrants. The building, restored in 1868, has a stunning hand-carved altarpiece filled with statuary.

➕ F18 ✉ Mott Street between Prince and Houston streets ☎ 212/226-8075 (call for times) 🕓 Sat–Sun, hours may vary 🚇 N, R, Prince Street 💲 Free

The dynamic New Museum

The Rubin Museum of Art

ST. PAUL'S CHAPEL

trinitywallstreet.org

Opened in 1766, this is the only remaining Colonial-era church in Manhattan. George Washington worshiped here after his inauguration. St. Paul's escaped destruction on 9/11 and became a round-the-clock refuge for rescue workers. In the churchyard is the Bell of Hope, a gift from the City of London on the first anniversary of the tragedy.

🚇 E21 ✉ 209 Broadway at Fulton Street
☎ 212/602-0800 🕐 Daily 10–6 🚇 2, 3, 4, 5, A, C, J, Z Fulton Street 💲 Free

SOUTH STREET SEAPORT

southstreetseaport.com
southstreetseaportmuseum.org

South Street Seaport is smaller than it once was, but still worth exploring. The South Street Seaport Museum traces the port's history from the 17th century and the collection includes historic ships you can board. Sailings are offered in summer. There are dining and shopping options here and an outpost of the Times Square TKTS ticket booth (▷ 56).

🚇 G21 ✉ Fulton Street at Water Street
☎ Museum 212/748-8600 🕐 Museum: Wed–Sun 11–7 🚇 2, 3, 4, 5, A, C, J, Z Fulton Street

SPYSCAPE

spyscape.com

This high-tech challenge is all about testing visitors' ability as spies, with kiosks that measure intelligence, personality and risk-taking potential. Exhibits chronicle spy landmarks like the Enigma code machine.

🚇 C10 ✉ 928 8th Avenue/55th Street
☎ 212/549-1941 🕐 Mon–Fri 10–9, Sat–Sun 9–9 🚇 C, E 50th Street; N, Q, R, W 57th Street 💲 Expensive

TENEMENT MUSEUM

tenement.org

This reconstruction of life in an 1863 tenement block is a must for history buffs. Guided tours of the tenement apartments focus on the homes and workshops of Jewish, Italian, Irish and later Puerto Rican and Polish immigrants who lived here. There are also walking tours of the neighborhood.

The Lightship Ambrose *at South Street Seaport*

🔲 G18 ✉ 103 Orchard Street
☎ 212/982-8420 🕐 Tours daily 10–5,
📍 F, J, M, Z Delancey Street–Essex Street;
B, D Grand Street 💰 Expensive

UNION SQUARE
Named for the union of Broadway
and Fourth Avenue, this is where
downtown and uptown meet. It is
ringed with shops and restaurants
and four days a week has the city's
best and biggest greenmarket,
selling homegrown produce
(▷ 125)—it's a great option for
a picnic lunch.
🔲 E15 ✉ E 14th–17th streets, Park
Avenue South, Broadway 🕐 Greenmarket
Mon, Wed, Fri, Sat 8–6 🍴 Numerous
📍 4, 5, 6, L, N, Q, R 14th Street–Union
Square 🚌 M3 ♿ Good

UNITED NATIONS HEADQUARTERS
visit.un.org
Take a guided tour to see the
General Assembly Hall and collection of art and artifacts donated
from around the world. A limited
number of same-day tickets are
available on site, but it's much
better to buy them online in
advance. Arrive at least one hour
early for security screening.
🔲 G11 ✉ 1st Avenue/45th–46th streets
☎ 212/963-8687 🕐 Mon–Fri 9–4.45
(a guided tour ticket is required) 🍴 Café,
restaurant 📍 4, 5, 6, 7 to Grand Central
💰 Expensive ❓ The Visitor Center (open
daily) is worth a stop; its shop features
products from all over the world. Also check
out Rodney Leon's "The Ark of Return," a
memorial to the victims of the slave trade

US CUSTOM HOUSE
nmai.si.edu/visit/newyork
Also known as the Alexander
Hamilton US Custom House, this

1907 Beaux Arts beauty, designed
by Cass Gilbert, now houses the
Smithsonian's National Museum of
the American Indian, highlighting
native cultures of North, Central
and South America. The permanent collection includes items from
ancient Paleo-Indian cultures to
contemporary arts; there are also
regular special exhibitions.
🔲 E23 ✉ 1 Bowling Green ☎ 212/514-
3700 🕐 Fri–Wed 10–5, Thu 10–8 📍 4, 5
Bowling Green; 1 South Ferry 💰 Free

WASHINGTON SQUARE
nycgovparks.org/parks/washington-
square-park
The square is a prime people-
watching spot in Greenwich
Village. At the north end,
Washington Memorial Arch,
designed by Stanford White, marks
the start of Fifth Avenue. Notice
"The Row" of Greek Revival homes
(Nos. 1–13) where the elite of
19th-century New York lived. If you
want to get a real feel, read Henry
James's *Washington Square*.
🔲 E17 📍 R, W 8th Street–NYU; A, B, C, D,
E, F, M 4th Street–Washington Square

The US Custom House

Farther Afield

BRONX ZOO

bronxzoo.com

The biggest city zoo in the US has more than 4,000 animals and is a leader in wildlife conservation. Don't miss the Congo Gorilla Forest, or the Wild Asia Complex with its monorail. There is also a new zipline that glides 45ft (13.7m) above the Bronx River.

See map ▷ 111 ✉ Fordham Road (Bronx River Parkway Northeast) ☎ 718/220-5100 ⏰ Apr–Oct daily 10–5; Nov–Mar 10–4.30 🍴 Restaurant, café 🚇 2 Pelham Parkway 💵 Expensive (Wed discounts)

THE CLOISTERS

metmuseum.org/visit/visit-the-cloisters

A 12th-century Spanish apse attached to a Romanesque cloister and a Gothic chapel—what's all this doing in Upper Manhattan? This is the Met's medieval branch. The bulk of the art and architecture, which is arranged chronologically, was amassed by sculptor George Grey Barnard in the early 20th century, much rescued from ruin.

See map ▷ 111 ✉ Fort Tryon Park, North Manhattan ☎ 212/923-3700 ⏰ Mar–Oct daily 10–5.15; Nov–Feb 10–4.45 🚇 A 190th Street 💵 Expensive (Met Museum admission includes entry to The Cloisters)

CONEY ISLAND

coneyisland.com

At the end of the 19th century, on a peak day Coney Island played host to a million people. Since then, attractions have come and gone but the big dipper ride, the Cyclone, is still here and Nathan's Famous hot dogs are still sold from the original site. MCU Park, home of the Brooklyn Cyclones baseball team, also hosts concerts. New amusement parks are revitalizing the area and the New York Aquarium has a spectacular new shark exhibit.

See map ▷ 110 ✉ Surf Avenue, Boardwalk; Aquarium: W 8th Street, Surf Avenue ☎ Aquarium 718/265-3474 ⏰ Jun–early Sep daily 10–5; Sep–May 10–3.30 🍴 Cafés 🚇 D, F, N, Q Coney Island–Stillwell Avenue 💵 Aquarium moderate, rides expensive

Bronx Zoo, the largest city zoo in the US

One of the set of late 15th-century Flemish Unicorn tapestries on display at The Cloisters

FLUSHING MEADOWS–CORONA PARK

nycgovparks.org

Queens' largest park has recreation facilities, the interactive New York Hall of Science (47-01 111th Street, tel 718/699-0005, nysci.org); the Queens Museum scale panorama of New York (New York Building, tel 718/592-9700, queensmuseum.org) and the Unisphere, the world's largest globe. Arthur Ashe Stadium hosts the US Open tennis tournament and the New York Mets play baseball at Citi Field.

➕ See map ▷ 111

HARLEM

This was the capital of black culture in America during the Harlem Renaissance in the 1920s. Music lovers should check out the Apollo Theater (253 W 125th Street, tel 212/531-5305, apollotheater.org) for big-name acts or the famous amateur showcase. Historic exhibits are mounted at the Schomburg Center for Research in Black Culture (515 Malcolm X Boulevard, tel 917/275-6975, nypl.org).

➕ See map ▷ 110

NEW YORK BOTANICAL GARDEN

nybg.org

America's largest city botanical center, a National Historic Landmark, has 250 acres (101ha) of beautiful displays every season. Floral extravaganzas, a fascinating conservatory and old growth trees are among the wonders.

➕ See map ▷ 111 ✉ 2900 Southern Boulevard, Bronx ☎ 718/817-8700
🎫 Daily 10–6

STATEN ISLAND

There are several historic sights here. Alice Austen House (2 Hylan Boulevard, tel 718/816-4506, aliceausten.org) is a museum of photographs by Alice Austen, one of America's earliest female photographers, in her colonial home. Historic Richmond Town (441 Clarke Avenue, tel 718/351-1611, historicrichmondtown.org) recreates daily life in a 19th-century village.

➕ See map ▷ 110

YANKEE STADIUM

yankees.mlb.com

The New York Yankees have been one of the most successful baseball teams in US history, since Babe Ruth joined them in 1920 and became a hero. Attending a game is a strong part of local culture and makes for a great night out.

➕ See map ▷ 111 ✉ E 161st Street, Bronx ☎ Tickets 877/469-9849 🎫 Season runs Apr–Oct. Check schedule for games
🍴 Concession stands 🚇 4, B, D 161st Street/Yankee Stadium 💲 Expensive

The Yankee Stadium in the Bronx, home of the New York Yankees

City Tours

This section contains self-guided tours that will help you explore the sights in each of the city's regions. Each tour is designed to take a day, with a map pinpointing the recommended places along the way. There is a quick reference guide at the end of each tour, listing everything you need in that region, so you know exactly what's close by.

CITY TOURS

Lower Manhattan

The cradle of New York, Lower Manhattan is steeped in history—new immigrants landed here from the 17th century until the early 20th century. This area is also home to the Financial District, historic Seaport and fashionable SoHo.

CITY TOURS

Morning
Start the day at the tip of Manhattan in **Battery Park** (▷ 66), with its splendid views of New York Harbor. Ferries for the **Statue of Liberty** (▷ 54–55) and **Ellis Island** (▷ 26–27) leave from Castle Clinton, but save these for a separate day. Cross State Street to admire the beautiful Beaux Arts facade of the **US Custom House** (▷ 73), housing the National Museum of the American Indian. Then proceed along Bowling Green, the small square opposite, past the Charging Bull statue (right), a symbol of Wall Street.

Mid-morning
Walk up Broadway and note the plaques for more than a century of ticker tape parades. Continue north to visit the **World Trade Center** (▷ 62–63). Farther south, **Trinity Church** (left; ▷ 59) marks the west end of **Wall Street** (▷ 58–59); stroll around the old churchyard, then head down Wall Street to **Federal Hall**, the **New York Stock Exchange** and other sites.

Lunch
Rub shoulders with Financial District workers and have a pub lunch at **The Bailey** (▷ 142), one block north of Wall Street. Try a hearty *plat du jour* such as shepherd's pie, fish and chips or Thai-spiced grilled shrimp.

Afternoon

Walk north on Front Street to **South Street Seaport** (▷ 72). From the waterfront along the East River there are good views of **Brooklyn Bridge** (▷ 66). Follow Dover Street west to **City Hall** (▷ 67), then take Centre Street north into **Chinatown** (left, ▷ 20–21). Explore its bustling markets, quiet temples and herbalist shops. Discover the culture of this area with a stop at the **Museum of Chinese in America** (▷ 70), which details the experiences of these immigrants.

Mid-afternoon

Chinatown spills north into **Little Italy**. Walk north on Mulberry Street, past the **Italian American Museum** (▷ 68), and when you reach **St. Patrick's Old Cathedral** (▷ 71), turn left on Prince Street, which will bring you into **SoHo** (▷ 52–53). Grab a coffee at **Dean & DeLuca** (▷ 52) to keep you going as you admire the cast-iron buildings and indulge in some shopping, from Nike to Saint Laurent. Most stores here stay open into early evening.

Evening

There are plenty of ultra-chic bars in SoHo for a cocktail or nightcap. For some old SoHo atmosphere, try **Fanelli's** (right, 94 Prince Street, between Mercer and Greene streets, tel 212/226-9412).

Dinner

After drinks, make your way east to **Delicatessen** (▷ 144), where they serve updated versions of classic comfort food. There's great SoHo people-watching from its outdoor tables. If you want something even more old-school, make **Lombardi's** (32 Spring Street at Mott Street, tel 212/941-7994) your destination. It was the first sit-down pizzeria in America.

Barrow Street
Morton Street
Leroy Street
Bedford Street
Leroy Street
Clarkson Street
Downing Street
Bleecker Street
Bleecker Street
Bleecker Street
NOLITA & NOHO
Broadway-Lafayette St

WEST HOUSTON STREET

Fanelli's

St Patrick's Old Cathedral

Children's Museum of the Arts

West Houston Street

Houston Street

King Street

Charlton Street

Vandam Street

Prince Street
Prince St
Delicatessen
Prince St
Elizabeth St

Dean & DeLuca

New Museum

Lombardi's

New York City Fire Museum

Spring Street

Dominick Street

SOHO

Spring
Spring St
Spring St

KENMARE STREET

Haughwout Building

BROOME STREET

Broome Street

Italian American Museum

Broome Street
LITTLE ITALY

WATTS STREET

CANAL STREET

Grand Street

Grand Street

Howard Street

Museum of Chinese in America

Canal Street
Holland Tunnel

CANAL STREET

Lispenard Street

Canal Street

Canal Street

WALKER STREET

CHINATOWN

TRIBECA

White Street

CANAL STREET

Orient Gallery

Franklin Street

Franklin Street

Leonard Street

Columbus Park

North Moore Street

Worth Street

Worth Street

Harrison Street

Thomas Street

CIVIC CENTER

NY State Supreme Court

Washington Market Park

Duane Street

Hogan Pl

Duane Street

Reade Street

Pearl Street

Chambers Street

Chambers Street

Chambers Street

Chambers St

Chambers Street

Warren Street

Chambers Street - World Trade Center

City Hall
City Hall Park

City Hall

Murray Street

Park Place

Brooklyn Bridge City Hall

World Financial Center

Park Place

World Trade Center

Murray Street

Barclay Street

Woolworth Building

Spruce Street

Frankfort Street

One World Observatory

Vesey Street

One World Trade Center

PATH

World Trade Center

St Paul's Chapel

Fulton

Beekman Street

Paulus Hook

Brookfield Place

TRANSPORTATION HUB

Fulton Street

FULTON CENTER TRANSIT HUB

Ann Street

National 9/11 Memorial & Museum

WTC Cortlandt

Dey St

Fulton St

Fulton Street

New York City Police Memorial

North Cove Yacht Harbor

Liberty Park

Cortlandt Street

John St

Maiden Lane

Platt Street

BATTERY PARK CITY

Liberty St

Albany Street

Cedar St

Federal Reserve Bank

Liberty St

FINANCIAL DISTRICT

The Bailey Pub & Brasserie

Albany St

Carlisle Street

Wall Street National Memorial

Wall
Street

Federal Hall

Pine Street

Rector Place

Trinity Church

Rector St

New York Stock Exchange

Broad Street

Wall St

Museum of American Finance

Rector Street

Wall Street

West Thames Street

Morris St

Delmonico's

3rd Place

Beaver Street

2nd Pl

Bowling Green

Stone Street

Bridge St

Vietnam Veterans Memorial

Museum of Jewish Heritage

1st Pl

BATTERY PL

US Custom House

STATE ST

Battery Park

Castle Clinton

Battery Park

East Coast Memorial

HUGH CAREY TUNNEL

South Ferry

Whitehall Street South Ferry

Staten Island Ferry Whitehall Terminal

Battery Maritime Building

Downtown Manhattan Heliport

Ellis Island

Governors Island

D   E   F

18 19 20 21 22 23

EAST HOUSTON STREET

Hamilton Fish Park

st 1st Street

EAST HOUSTON STREET

Stanton Street

Stanton Street

Eldridge Street

Ludlow Street

Essex Street

Norfolk Street

Suffolk Street

Clinton Street

Attorney Street

Ridge Street

Pitt Street

Columbia Street

Rivington Street

FDR DRIVE

Stanton Street

ALLEN STREET

ESSEX STREET

Delancey Street

WILLIAMSBURG BRIDGE

Delancey Street Essex Street

DELANCEY STREET

DELANCEY STREET

NORFOLK ST

Clinton Street

Suffolk Street

Broome Street

Baruch Place

Abraham Place

Lewis Street

FDR DRIVE

Tenement Museum

Orchard Street

Essex Street

GRAND

STREET

Thompson Plaza

LOWER EAST SIDE

Grand Street

Hester Street

Forsyth Street

Allen Street

Eldridge Street

Orchard Street

Ludlow Street

Seward Park

East Broadway

Henry Street

Madison Street

Jackson Street

Cherry Street

Corlears Hook Park

Corlears Hook

E 34th Street/Midtown

Hester Street

Canal Street

East Broadway

Eldridge Street Synagogue

Forsyth St

Broadway

Henry Street

Jefferson Street

Rutgers Street

Clinton Street

Montgomery Street

Water Street

Front Street

Pier 42 Park

Division

East

Market Street

PIKE STREET

Henry Street

Cherry Street

SOUTH STREET

Schaefer Landing/ S Williamsburg

Henry Street

Catharine Street

Monroe Street

Madison Street

Cherry Street

Water Street

FRANKLIN D. ROOSEVELT (FDR) DRIVE

East River

er E Wagner Snr Pl

MANHATTAN BRIDGE

VINEGAR HILL

John St.

er Street

Brooklyn Bridge

BROOKLYN

BRIDGE

Brooklyn Bridge Park

John Street

Plymouth Street

Hudson Avenue

Gold Street

Adams Street

Jay Street

Water Street

Front Street

ck Slip

lon

ket

FDR DRIVE

South Street Seaport

Empire-Fulton Ferry State Park

Water Street

Front Street

York Street

York Street

DUMBO

278

Brooklyn Bridge Park/ DUMBO

Old Fulton Street

Doughty Street

FULTON FERRY

Poplar Street

High Street

Adams Street

Jay Street

Pier 11 all Street ermial

Furman Street

Middagh Street

Cranberry Street

Orange Street

Pineapple Street

Henry Street

Hicks Street

Cadman Plaza Park

CADMAN PLAZA WEST

Courthouse

TILLARY STREET

Post Office

Johnson Street

ADAMS STREET

BROOKLYN-QUEENS EXPRESSWAY

Columbia Heights

Willow Street

Clark Street

Clark Street

Monroe Place

NY State Supreme Court

Court Street

BROOKLYN HEIGHTS

Love Lane

Brooklyn Historical Society

Clinton Street

Pierrepont Street

Brooklyn Borough Hall

Brooklyn Bridge Park

Montague Terr

Montague Street

Hicks Street

Remsen Street

Henry Street

Hunts La

COURT ST

BROOKLYN

Grace Court

Grace Ct. Alley

278

0   500 m

0   500 yds

aulus look

Rockaway

Belford/ Harbor Way

Governors Island

Bay Ridge

G   H   J

Lower Manhattan Quick Reference Guide

TOP 25 SIGHTS AND EXPERIENCES

Chinatown (▷ 20)
Explore this bustling neighborhood of streetside produce stalls, herbalist shops, Buddhist temples, dim sum parlors and tempting restaurants.

Ellis Island (▷ 26)
Follow in the footsteps of millions of immigrants, most of whom traveled in cramped steerage class, who passed through this gateway to New York and the New World.

SoHo (▷ 52)
SoHo features unique boutiques, top clothing chains, several art galleries, fashionable bars and stylish restaurants in 19th-century cast-iron buildings.

Statue of Liberty (▷ 54)
A visit to this iconic landmark is a must on any trip to New York. The ferry ride to the island is impressive, and the view from the statue's crown is breathtaking.

Wall Street (▷ 58)
During Dutch colonial times, Wall Street marked the northern boundary of New York. Now home to bankers and brokers, it's the powerhouse of the US economy.

World Trade Center (▷ 62)
The National September 11 Memorial, on the site of the Twin Towers, is both impressive and poignant. It's a quiet place for peace and contemplation.

CITY TOURS

Downtown and Chelsea

The area from Houston Street north to 30th Street encompasses NoHo and the East Village, the tree-lined streets of Greenwich Village, the Meatpacking District with its fashionable stores and clubs, and Chelsea, home of the High Line and the Whitney Museum of American Art.

Morning
Start the day with breakfast at one of the bakeries in **Chelsea Market** (right; ▷ 121). You can either eat there or take it with you up to the **High Line** (▷ 40–41). Begin your explorations on this converted railbed by heading north, but eventually find your way to the Gansevoort Street end of the park and the **Whitney Museum of American Art** (▷ 60–61).

Late morning/lunch
Leave the High Line at its southern terminus and strike out for the heart of **Greenwich Village** (▷ 36–37) along Bleecker Street. If you need a snack, you'll pass **Magnolia Bakery** (401 Bleecker Street), made (in)famous by the TV show *Sex and the City*. When Bleecker Street reaches MacDougal Street, head north. These blocks were the epicenter of the early 1960s folk scene. You'll soon reach **Washington Square** (▷ 73) which is a great place for people-watching. But first, lunch—the bistro-style **North Square Restaurant** (▷ 147) in the **Washington Square Hotel** (▷ 159) is a good choice for Mediterranean dishes.

Afternoon
After lunch, stroll through Washington Square to its southern side (West 4th Street) and begin walking east to the **East Village** (▷ 24–25). The **Merchant's House Museum** is a fascinating look back at an earlier era, complete with furnishings that were moved into the house in the 1830s. Then make your way up to **St. Mark's Place** (E 8th Street) with its lively mix of ethnic restaurants and funky shops.

CITY TOURS

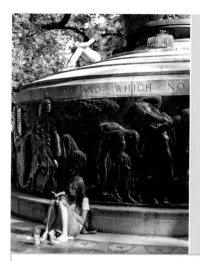

Late afternoon
From the East Village head back to Broadway and the **Strand Bookstore** (▷ 125) and **Grace Church**, which has free audio tours via cell phone. Just a few blocks north of the church is **Union Square** (left, ▷ 73). Visit on a Monday, Wednesday, Friday or Saturday, and you'll be able to browse the food stands of **Union Square Greenmarket** (▷ 125).

Evening
For a historic watering hole, head for the **White Horse Tavern** (▷ 137) on Hudson Street, where poet Dylan Thomas drank his last. Or head up to 23rd Street: At Fifth Avenue is **Eataly** (▷ 121), which has imported Italian goods and fine restaurants. It stands in the shadow of the **Flatiron Building** (▷ 68), New York's best early skyscraper.

Dinner
If you're not dining at Eataly, head a few blocks north to **Pondicheri** (▷ 148), a sophisticated take on classic Indian dishes with an emphasis on sharing.

Late evening
After dinner, you are spoiled for choice. Return to the Meatpacking District (right) or head back to the West Village for jazz at the **Blue Note** (▷ 132) or the **Village Vanguard** (178 7th Avenue South at W 11th Street, tel 212/255-4037). The clubs on Bleecker and MacDougal Street feature live music, too, with **Le Poisson Rouge** (158 Bleecker Street, tel 212/505-3474) drawing a wide range of acts, from classical trios to world music to cult bands.

Midtown W 39th St

West 39th Street
West 38th Street
LINCOLN TUNNEL 495
West 37th Street
GARMENT
DISTRICT
12
Jacob Javits
Convention
Center
West 36th Street
Pier 76
West 35th Street
14th Street
Penn Station
Macy's
WEST 34TH STREET
14th Street
Penn Station
14th Street
Herald Square
West 33rd Street
West 31st Street
HUDSON
YARDS
The
Vessel
Hudson
Yards
Retail
Madison
Square
Garden
PENN
STATION
13
West 30th
Street
Heliport
WEST 30TH STREET
West 30th Street
West 29th Street
West 28th Street
28th Street
Chelsea
Park
West 27th Street
CHELSEA
GALLERY
DISTRICT
West 26th Street
MANHATTAN
West 25th Street
14
High Line
West 24th Street
CHELSEA
West 23rd Street
23rd Street
West 23rd
23rd Street
Chelsea
Waterside
Park
West 22nd Street
West 21st Street
Chelsea Hotel
West 20th Street
West 19th Street
West 18th Street
18th Street
15
Chelsea Piers
West 17th Street
West 16th Street
Rubin Museum
of Art
N
Chelsea Market
West 15th Street
MEATPACKING
DISTRICT
14th Street
14th Street
14th St
WEST 14TH STREET
8th Avenue
6th Avenue
West 13th Street
Little West 12th Street
WEST
VILLAGE
Village
Vanguard
16
Whitney Museum
of American Art
Jane Street
Magnolia
Bakery
West 12th Street
Bethune Street
White Horse
Tavern
Bank Street
Christopher Street
Sheridan Square
West Washington
West 4th Street
GREENWICH
VILLAGE
John's Pizza
17
Hudson River
West 10th Street
Christopher Street
Bleecker Street
Barrow Street
Morton Street
Leroy Street
Leroy Street
Clarkson Street
Houston
Street
King Street
18
West Houston Street
Children's
Museum
of the Arts
Charlton Street
VARICK STREET
B
Pier 40
C
New York City
Fire Museum
D
Spring

CITY TOURS

86

East 39th Street
East 38th Street
East 37th Street
GREATOWN
East 36th Street
East 35th Street

Morgan Library & Museum

34TH STREET   EAST 34TH STREET   EAST 34TH STREET

E 34th St Midtown

East 34th Street Heliport

Empire State Building

East 33rd Street   33rd Street   East 33rd Street

East 32nd Street   East 32nd Street

MIDTOWN SOUTH

West 31st Street   East 31st Street   East 31st Street   KIPS BAY

West 30th Street   East 30th Street   East 30th Street

East River

West 29th Street   East 29th Street   East 29th Street

8th Street   East 28th Street   28th Street   East 28th Street

Pondicheri   East 27th Street   East 27th Street

East 26th St   East 26th Street   East 26th Street

SkyPort Seaplane Terminal

East 25th St   East 25th Street   East 25th Street

Madison Square Park

East 24th St   East 24th Street   East 24th Street

FLATIRON DISTRICT   23rd Street   East 23rd Street   23rd Street   East 23rd Street

Eataly   **Flatiron Building**   East 22nd Street   East 22nd Street

East 22nd Street   East 21st Street   East 21st Street

East 21st Street   *Theodore Roosevelt Birthplace*   *Gramercy Park*   **GRAMERCY**

East 20th Street   East 20th Street

East 19th Street   **Union Square Cafe**   East 19th Street   East 19th Street

East 18th Street   *Block Beautiful*   East 18th Street   East 18th Street

East 17th Street   **Union Square**   East 17th Street   **STUYVESANT TOWN**

East 16th Street   *Irving Place*   East 16th St

East 15th Street   **UNION SQUARE**   *Stuyvesant Square*   East 15th Street

Union Square Park

EAST 14TH ST   EAST 14TH STREET   3rd Avenue   EAST 14TH STREET   1st Avenue

14th Street–Union Square

East 13th Street   **Strand Bookstore**   East 13th Street

East 12th Street   East 12th Street   East 12th Street

East 11th Street   East 11th Street   East 11th Street

Grace Church

East 10th Street   East 10th St   **EAST VILLAGE AND NOHO**

East 9th Street   East 9th Street

8th Street–NYU   St Marks Place

North Square Restaurant   East 8th Street   *Tompkins Square Park*

Washington Square   Astor Place–Cooper Union   East 7th Street

Waverly Place   East 6th Street   **ALPHABET CITY**

Washington Square Park   East 5th Street

4th Street Washington Sq   *The Ukranian Museum*

West 4th Street   *Merchant's House Museum*   East 4th Street

Blue Note   West 3rd Street   Great Jones Street   East 3rd Street

Bond Street   East 2nd Street

Bleecker Street   *Bleecker Street*   East 1st Street   EAST HOUSTON STREET

NOLITA

WEST HOUSTON STREET   Broadway–Lafayette Street   Jersey St

St Patrick's Old Cathedral   Stanton

Prince Street   Prince Street   **New Museum**   Rivington

(E)   St   (F)   Spring Street   (G)

Spring Street   Bowery

SOHO   **Tenement Museum**

0   500 m
0   500 yds

Downtown and Chelsea
Quick Reference Guide

CITY TOURS

East Village and NoHo (▷ 24)
The East Village, with its immigrant history and counterculture vibe, is well worth exploring. Nearby NoHo, once one of the most elegant residential neighborhoods in the city, still features beautiful homes and cobblestone streets.

Greenwich Village (▷ 36)
Once an actual village, this area has gorgeous, tree-lined streets. It was the center of the folk revival of the 1960s and birthplace of the gay rights movement, and has been home to generations of artists and writers.

High Line (▷ 40)
Local residents banded together to turn this abandoned elevated railbed into one of New York's premier parks. Watch for the Plinth, due to open in 2019 and inspired by London's Trafalgar Square Fourth Plinth, with commissioned art.

Whitney Museum of American Art (▷ 60)
One of the finest collections of 20th-century American art. Enjoy stimulating temporary exhibitions alongside works from the outstanding permanent collection.

Midtown

Midtown is a must for visitors. It has leading museums, pulsating Times Square, Grand Central Terminal plus the magnet for shoppers—Fifth Avenue. It also has three of New York's most famous skyscrapers, two with observatories for stupendous views.

Morning

Get an early start at **Rockefeller Center** (▷ 50–51). The subway concourse below 30 Rockefeller Plaza is full of restaurants, cafés and delis; pick up a coffee and breakfast sandwich, or have a more substantial meal at the **Rock Center Café**, which looks out on the famous ice rink or summer gardens. Be sure to see the many beautiful artworks around the complex, before or after enjoying the observation decks at **Top of the Rock** (right) for majestic city views.

Mid-morning

Walk west along 50th Street to **Radio City Music Hall** (▷ 136), and turn right up Sixth Avenue. Turn right on 53rd Street to visit the **Museum of Modern Art** (▷ 46–47).

Lunch

"Quick" and "inexpensive" are foreign words in this part of Midtown. Your best bet for a simple lunch that won't break the bank is to head to the **Halal Guys**, who operate their renowned food carts at the corner of 53rd Street and Avenue of the Americas. Or splurge at **Norma's** (in the Parker Meridien at 119 W 56th Street), which serves one of the city's most expensive breakfasts.

Afternoon

Walk east to **Fifth Avenue** (▷ 30–31) and let the shopping spree begin—even if you're just window shopping and ogling the fabulous displays. If you enter only one store, make it **Saks Fifth Avenue** (▷ 125); the perfume and cosmetic counters fill the first floor. Just north is the beautiful **St. Patrick's Cathedral** (▷ 71).

Mid-afternoon

Turn east on 45th Street and walk to the Park Avenue entrance of **Grand Central Terminal** (▷ 34–35). Admire its stunning main concourse, then head downstairs for a welcome rest and a snack in the **Dining Concourse** (▷ 145). Exit on 42nd Street, and detour one block east to step into the art deco lobby of the **Chrysler Building** (▷ 67). Then walk west on 42nd Street to Fifth Avenue, and visit the **New York Public Library** (left; ▷ 48–49).

Evening

As dusk falls, continue west and turn right up Broadway into **Times Square** (▷ 56–57), in all its neon glory. Head for the **TKTS booth** (▷ 56), where you may get a discount ticket for a Broadway show.

Dinner

Times Square is notorious for chain restaurants, but a good choice for real New York fare is **John's Pizzeria** (▷ 146). There's a branch of **Carmine's** at 200 W 44th Street, off Times Square.

Late evening

Afterward, take in that Broadway show, and/or grab a cab to end the evening with the best nightcap of all: the view of the twinkling lights of Manhattan from the top of the **Empire State Building** (right; ▷ 28–29).

Coliseum Park
Time Warner Center
Columbus Circle
59th Street Columbus Circle
The Pond
Central Park South
5th Ave 59th St

⑨ West 58th St
Museum of Arts and Design (MAD)
57th Street
West 58th Street

WEST 57TH STREET
57th Street
WEST 57TH STREET
Tr To

Columbus Avenue
Carnegie Hall
Parker Meridien Hotel
West 56th Street
West 56th Street

West 55th Street
MIDTOWN
West 55th Street
Museum of Modern Art
5th Avenue

Spyscape
Halal Guys
West 54th Street

West 53rd Street
7th Avenue
5th Ave 53rd St

⑩ West 52nd Street
West 52nd Street

West 51st Street
West 51st Street
St Patrick's Cathedral

Radio City Music Hall
'wichcraft, Rock Center Café

9th Avenue
West 50th Street
50th Street
50th Street
7th Avenue
Rockefeller Center

CitizenM Hotel
8th Avenue
49th Street

West 49th Street
47th-50th Streets Rockefeller Ctr
West 48th Street
Sa Fi Av

West 48th Street
THEATER DISTRICT
West 47th Street

West 47th Street
TKTS booth
West 46th Street

West 46th Street
Times Square
West 45th Street

⑪ West 45th Street
National Geographic Encounter: Ocean Odyssey
Fifth Avenue

West 44th Street
Carmine's
Gulliver's Gate
West 44th Street
MIDTOWN

West 43rd Street
42nd Street Port Authority Bus Terminal
Reuters Building
Times Square 42nd Street
West 43rd Street

WEST 42ND STREET
5th Aver
WEST 42ND STREET

Port Authority Bus Terminal
New Amsterdam Theater
New York Public Library

West 40th Street
Bryant Park
West 40th Street

West 39th Street
West 39th Street

⑫ West 38th Street
8th Avenue
7th Avenue
Broadway
6th Avenue
5th Avenue
West 38th Street

West 37th Street
GARMENT DISTRICT
West 37th Street
KOREATOWN

9th Avenue
West 36th Street
West 36th Street

West 35th Street
West 35th Street

34th Street Penn Station
WEST 34TH STREET
Macy's
WEST 34TH STREET

West 33rd Street
34th Street Penn Station
34th Street Herald Square
West 33rd Street
Empire State Building

⑬ Madison Square Garden
PENN STATION
West 32nd Street
MIDTOWN SOUTH

West 31st Street
West 31st Street

Ⓒ West 30th Street
Ⓓ West 30th Street

60th Street
Lexington Avenue/59th Street
East 60th Street
59th Street
Forty Carrots
East 59th Street
EAST 59TH STREET
SUTTON PLACE
SUTTON PL
59th Street
58th Street
East 58th Street
ST 57TH STREET
EAST 57TH STREET
Sutton Place South
56th Street
East 56th Street
55th Street
East 55th Street
MIDTOWN EAST
t 54th Street
East 54th Street
Lexington Avenue/
53rd Street
Lipstick
Building
East 53rd Street
t 53rd Street
TURTLE
BAY
Seagram
Building
East 52nd Street
t 52nd St
5 lst
Street
East 51st Street
t 51st St
Park Avenue
Lexington Avenue
3RD AVENUE
2ND AVENUE
1ST AVENUE
50th St
Pod Hotel
East 50th Street
Beekman Place
49th St
East 49th Street
Mitchell Pl
48th St
East 48th Street
t 47th Street
East 47th Street
46th Street
East 46th Street
45th Street
East 45th Street
United Nations
Headquarters
Grand
Central
Terminal
4th St
East 44th Street
East River
3rd St
East 43rd Street
TUDOR
CITY
Chrysler
Building
ST 42ND ST
EAST 42ND STREET
42nd Street -
Grand Central
Daily News
Building
t 41st Street
Chanin
Building
East 41st Street
FRANKLIN D. ROOSEVELT (FDR) DRIVE
t 40th Street
MURRAY HILL
East 40th Street
Madison Avenue
Park Avenue
Lexington Avenue
3RD AVENUE
2ND AVENUE
1ST AVENUE
39th St
East 39th Street
38th St
East 38th Street
N
37th St
Morgan Library
& Museum
st 36th Street
35th Street
E 34th St/
Midtown
ST 34TH STREET
EAST 34TH STREET
st 33rd St
East 33rd Street
33rd Street
0   500 m
East
34th Street
Heliport
st 32nd St
0   500 yds
Park Avenue S
ast 31st St
KIPS BAY
E
F
East 30th Street
G

SIGHTS AND EXPERIENCES

Empire State Building (▷ 28)
The most famous New York sky-scraper affords panoramic views over Manhattan by day or night.

Fifth Avenue (▷ 30)
For high fashion, style and quality, there's no better place to shop than Fifth Avenue.

Grand Central Terminal (▷ 34)
Some half a million people pass through this stunning Beaux Arts concourse every day.

Museum of Modern Art (▷ 46)
From 19th-century masterpieces to contemporary art, this is one of the city's leading museums.

New York Public Library (▷ 48)
See the fine carved ceiling and the glorious reading rooms of this Beaux Arts landmark.

Rockefeller Center (▷ 50)
Admire the plaza and artworks of this urban complex, then take in the view from the Top of the Rock.

Times Square (▷ 56)
Come here at night to see the wall of neon at the heart of New York's famous Theater District or browse in its megastores by day.

CITY TOURS

MORE TO SEE 64

Chrysler Building
Gulliver's Gate
Morgan Library & Museum
National Geographic Encounter: Ocean Odyssey
St. Patrick's Cathedral
Spyscape
United Nations Headquarters

SHOP 114

Clothes
Brooks Brothers
Dolce & Gabbana
Thomas Pink
Department Stores
Bergdorf Goodman
Macy's
Saks Fifth Avenue

Shoes
Manolo Blahnik
Sports Goods
Niketown
Technology
Apple Store

ENTERTAINMENT 126

Bars
Four Seasons Hotel TY Bar
Classical Music
Carnegie Hall
Jazz
Birdland
Live Music
Madison Square Garden
PlayStation Theater

Theater/Performance
The New Victory Theater
New World Stages
Radio City Music Hall
Signature Theatre
TV Show Recording
The Tonight Show starring
    Jimmy Fallon

EAT 138

Asian
Kajitsu
Nobu Fifty Seven
Casual
Forty Carrots
John's Pizzeria
Classic NY
'21' Club
Oyster Bar

Fine Dining
Le Bernardin
Casa Lever
Per Se
Greek
Uncle Nick's

CITY TOURS

Upper East Side and Central Park

Central Park is a huge green space accessible to all New Yorkers. The museums of the Upper East Side, facing the park along Fifth Avenue, are renowned worldwide. Their collections range from priceless antiquities to modern art, design, ethnic culture and history.

Morning
It's unlikely you'll visit more than two museums in a day. This tour will take you past the most popular, and give you a taste of Central Park in between. Most museums don't open until 10am, so start with an early morning stroll in **Central Park** (left; ▷ 18–19). Enter at the southeast corner by Grand Army Plaza (E 59th Street and Fifth Avenue). A pedestrian path (just in from Fifth Avenue) leads to the zoo. If you follow the paved road, first detour to the Pond, with lovely views of the skyline, before reaching the Dairy Visitor Center, where you can pick up a park map. Continue north along The Mall, lined with one of the largest stands of elm trees in America. The southern end, Literary Walk, has statues of famous writers.

Mid-morning
Just before the Naumburg Bandshell, veer right and follow paths to exit the park at 69th Street. Go one block north to visit the **Frick Collection** (▷ 32–33). Otherwise, continue through the park to the Bethesda Terrace and Fountain (right), overlooking the Lake. Admire the view, then take the pedestrian walkway beneath the terrace—look up to see the Minton tile ceiling, designed by British architect Jacob Wrey Mould. Follow the lakeside path to your right. At Loeb Boathouse veer right to the Conservatory Water, the pretty model boat pond.

Lunch
The Met, Guggenheim, Cooper Hewitt and Neue Galerie all have cafés. In Central Park, **The Loeb Boathouse** restaurant (▷ 147) has an express café as well as formal dining on the terrace. Alternatively, picnic on the Great Lawn behind the Met.

Afternoon
A visit to the **Metropolitan Museum of Art** (left; ▷ 44–45) is worthwhile. It stands right in Central Park. Try to catch a free tour of the museum's highlights (times vary). At Fifth Avenue and 86th Street is the **Neue Galerie** (▷ 70). Farther north at 89th Street is the **Guggenheim Museum** (▷ 38–39), housed in Frank Lloyd Wright's stunning circular building. Beyond is the **Cooper Hewitt Smithsonian Design Museum** (▷ 22–23) and the **Jewish Museum** (▷ 68). Across Fifth Avenue in Central Park is the famous Reservoir. The running track and bridle path around the Reservoir are good places to stroll.

Evening
In summer, Central Park has evening events (Shakespeare in the Park; concerts on the Great Lawn), but be aware of your surroundings when in the park after dark. If a museum has a late night, evenings are a good time to visit, or head for a cocktail at upscale **Bemelmans Bar** (Carlyle Hotel, 35 E 76th Street, tel 212/744-1600).

Dinner
The superb (and pricey) French cuisine at nearby **Café Boulud** (▷ 143) makes it a good choice for dinner.

Late evening
Return to Carlyle Hotel's **Café Carlyle** (▷ 132) for jazz and cabaret.

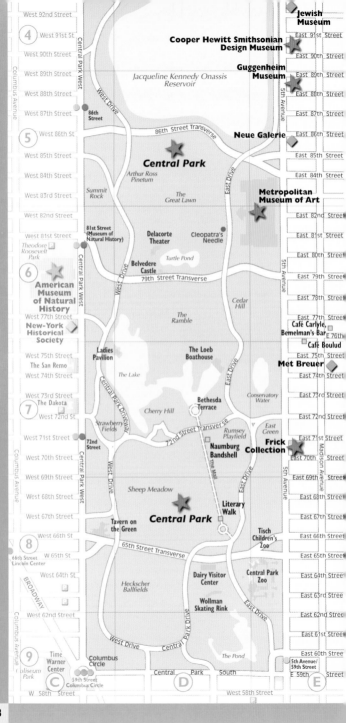

CITY TOURS

Jewish Museum

Cooper Hewitt Smithsonian Design Museum

Guggenheim Museum

Neue Galerie

Metropolitan Museum of Art

Central Park

American Museum of Natural History

New-York Historical Society

Met Breuer

Café Carlyle, Bemelman's Bar

Café Boulud

Frick Collection

Central Park

West 92nd Street
West 91st Street
West 90th Street
West 89th Street
West 88th Street
West 87th Street
West 86th St
West 85th Street
West 84th Street
West 83rd Street
West 82nd Street
West 81st Street
West 77th Street
West 75th Street
West 74th Street
West 73rd Street
West 72nd St
West 71st Street
West 70th Street
West 69th Street
West 68th Street
West 67th Street
West 66th St
W 65th St
West 64th St
West 62nd Street

Columbus Avenue

Central Park West

Theodore Roosevelt Park

The San Remo

The Dakota

66th Street Lincoln Center

BROADWAY

Time Warner Center

Coliseum Park

Columbus Circle

59th Street Columbus Circle

W 58th Street

West Drive

86th Street Transverse

Arthur Ross Pinetum

Summit Rock

The Great Lawn

81st Street (Museum of Natural History)

Delacorte Theater

Cleopatra's Needle

Turtle Pond

Belvedere Castle

79th Street Transverse

Cedar Hill

The Ramble

Ladies Pavilion

The Loeb Boathouse

The Lake

Conservatory Water

Cherry Hill

Bethesda Terrace

Strawberry Fields

72nd Street Transverse

Rumsey Playfield

East Green

72nd Street

Naumburg Bandshell

The Mall

Sheep Meadow

Literary Walk

Tavern on the Green

Tisch Children's Zoo

65th Street Transverse

Heckscher Ballfields

Dairy Visitor Center

Central Park Zoo

Wollman Skating Rink

West Drive

Central Park Drive

East Drive

The Pond

Central Park South

Central Park

Jacqueline Kennedy Onassis Reservoir

Central Park Driveway

East Drive

5th Avenue

Madison Avenue

East 91st Street
East 90th Street
East 89th Street
East 88th Street
East 87th Street
East 86th Street
East 85th Street
East 84th Street
East 82nd Street
East 81st Street
East 80th Street
East 79th Street
East 78th Street
East 77th Street
E 76th St
East 75th Street
East 74th Street
East 73rd Street
East 72nd Street
East 71st Street
East 70th Street
East 69th Street
East 68th Street
East 67th Street
East 66th Street
East 65th Street
East 64th Street
East 63rd Street
East 62nd Street
East 61st Street
East 60th Street
5th Avenue/ 59th Street
E 59th Street

4

5

6

7

8

9

C

D

E

East 92nd Street
East 91st Street
East 90th Street
East 89th Street
East 88th Street
East 87th Street
East 86th Street
East 85th Street
East 84th Street
East 83rd Street
East 82nd Street
East 81st Street
East 80th Street
East 79th Street
East 78th Street
East 77th Street
East 76th Street
East 75th Street
East 74th Street
East 73rd Street
East 72nd Street
East 71st Street
East 70th Street
East 69th Street
East 68th Street
East 67th Street
East 66th Street
East 65th Street
East 64th Street
EAST 63RD STREET
EAST 62ND STREET
East 61st Street
EAST 59TH STREET
East 58th Street

FRANKLIN D. ROOSEVELT (FDR) DRIVE

Carl Schurz Park

East End Avenue

Lexington Avenue
3RD AVENUE
2ND AVENUE
1ST AVENUE
YORK AVENUE

UPPER EAST SIDE

72nd Street

Asia Society and Museum

Hunter College

68th Street Hunter College

St Catherine's Park

LENOX HILL

Rockefeller University

East River

Roosevelt Island

Road 5

Lexington Avenue/63rd Street

Lexington Avenue/59th Street

59th Street

Roosevelt Island Aerial Tramway
QUEENSBORO BRIDGE

86th Street
86th Street
77th Street

SUTTON PLACE

F   G   H

0   250 m
0   250 yds

N

Upper East Side and Central Park
Quick Reference Guide

CITY TOURS

Central Park (▷ 18)
This great, green expanse is a visionary creation in the heart of the city. Join New Yorkers as they walk, jog, cycle, row, picnic, stroll with their dogs, play ball and escape the urban buzz.

Cooper Hewitt Smithsonian Design Museum (▷ 22)
An eclectic mix of old-school and cutting-edge, the superb exhibits and permanent collections of furniture and decorative arts in the Carnegie mansion are stunning.

Frick Collection (▷ 32)
The mansion of this 19th-century robber baron is worth a visit in itself, and forms a splendid backdrop for his magnificent collection of old masters and decorative arts.

Guggenheim Museum (▷ 38)
Frank Lloyd Wright's ground-breaking, nautilus-shaped building with its internal spiral walkway gets all the glory, but the collection of late19th- and 20th-century art is also worth a look.

Metropolitan Museum of Art (▷ 44)
Don't be daunted by the sheer vastness of this fabulous art museum. Viewing just one or two of its wonderful collections will leave lasting memories.

MORE TO SEE   64

Jewish Museum
Met Breuer
El Museo del Barrio
Museum of the City of New York
Neue Galerie

SHOP   114

Books
Kitchen Arts and Letters
Clothes
Calvin Klein
Ralph Lauren

Department Stores
Barneys
Bloomingdale's

ENTERTAINMENT   126

Bars
Auction House
Comedy
Dangerfield's
Jazz
Café Carlyle

Literary Events/Readings
92nd Street Y
Theater/Performance
Florence Gould Hall
Shakespeare in the Park

EAT   138

Casual
Jackson Hole
Classic NY
The Loeb Boathouse
Fine Dining
Daniel

French
Café Boulud
Middle Eastern
A La Turka
Persepolis

Upper West Side

The area west of Central Park is a largely residential, pleasantly leafy neighborhood of grand apartment buildings and big brownstones. Its major attractions are Lincoln Center and the wonderful American Museum of Natural History.

Morning

Start at **Lincoln Center** (▷ 42–43). Walk around the plaza, admiring the Revson Fountain, the Metropolitan Opera House and other cultural venues. Guided tours are available from the David Rubenstein Atrium across Broadway. From the northeast corner of the Lincoln Center, cross over the intersection with Broadway to the **American Folk Art Museum** (left; ▷ 66). Continue up Columbus Avenue, taking in its shops and restaurants. If you're ready for a snack, you'll pass the **Magnolia Bakery** (200 Columbus Avenue)—it's never too early for one of their cupcakes.

Mid-morning

Turn right on W 72nd Street. On the corner with Central Park West is the Dakota, the first luxury co-op apartment building on the Upper West Side. Its most famous resident, former Beatle John Lennon, was fatally shot outside the south gate in 1980. Cross over the road to enter **Central Park** (▷ 18–19), and follow the path to **Strawberry Fields**, where the black-and-white *Imagine* mosaic (right) is the centerpiece of a garden and memorial to John Lennon. From here there is a good view of the Dakota Apartments and the towers of the neighboring San Remo Apartments. Farther on is the **New-York Historical Society** (▷ 70–71). Cross back to Central Park West and continue on 73rd Street to Broadway.

Lunch

Broadway is another great shopping street. Continue north to 80th Street, where you can put together a picnic from the gourmet fare at **Zabar's** (right; ▷ 125), or get a sandwich at their adjoining café. Take it to **Riverside Park**, two blocks west, with views over the Hudson River.

Afternoon

Plan to spend the entire afternoon at the **American Museum of Natural History** (▷ 14–15). Highlights include the dinosaur halls, the animal dioramas, the Rose Center for Earth and Space (left) and more.

Dinner

You won't have too much further to walk for an early dinner at **Blossom on Columbus** (▷ 143), the uptown outpost of this beloved vegetarian mini-chain, which emphasizes seasonal ingredients.

Evening

End where you started by retracing your steps back to **Lincoln Center** (right). Even if you haven't got tickets for an evening performance, a walk through the lit-up plaza is a magical way to end the day.

West 90th Street
West 89th Street
West 88th Street
West 87th Street
West 86th Street
West 85th Street
West 84th Street
West 83rd Street
West 82nd Street
West 81st Street
West 80th Street
West 79th Street
West 78th Street
West 77th Street
West 76th Street
West 75th Street
West 74th Street
West 73rd Street
West 72nd Street
West 71st Street
West 70th Street
West 69th Street
West 68th Street
West 67th Street
West 66th Street
West 65th Street
West 64th Street
West 63rd Street
West 62nd Street
West 61st Street
West 60th Street
West 59th Street
West 58th Street
WEST 57TH STREET

HENRY HUDSON PARKWAY
Riverside Drive
West End Avenue
BROADWAY
Amsterdam Avenue
Columbus Avenue
Central Park West

86th Street
86th Street
81st Street (Museum of Natural History)
79th Street
72nd Street
72nd Street
66th Street Lincoln Center
59th St Columbus
Columbus Circle

Riverside Park
Hudson River
JOE DIMAGGIO HIGHWAY
Riverside Boulevard
Freedom Place

Blossom on Columbus
Zabar's
Theodore Roosevelt Park
American Museum of Natural History
New-York Historical Society
The San Remo
The Dakota
Ansonia Building
UPPER WEST SIDE
Magnolia Bakery
American Folk Art Museum
Juilliard School
Lincoln Center
Damrosch Park
LINCOLN SQUARE
Fordham University Lincoln Center Campus
Time Warner Center
Coliseum Park
Museum of Arts and Design (MAD)

N

4
5
6
7
8
9

A
B
C

Cooper Hewitt Smithsonian
Design Museum

East 90th Street

Guggenheim
Museum

East 89th Street

East 88th Street

East 87th Street

Jacqueline Kennedy Onassis
Reservoir

86th Street

Neue Galerie

East 86th Street

86th Street Transverse

East 85th Street

Central Park

East 84th Street

Arthur Ross
Pinetum

The
Great Lawn

Metropolitan
Museum of Art

East 82nd Street

East 81st Street

Delacorte
Theater

Cleopatra's
Needle

East 80th Street

Belvedere
Castle

Turtle Pond

East 79th Street

79th Street Transverse

East 78th Street

Cedar
Hill

East 77th Street

77th Street

The
Ramble

East 76th Street

East 75th Street

Ladies
Pavilion

The Loeb
Boathouse

East 74th Street

The Lake

East 73rd Street

Conservatory
Water

UPPER EAST SIDE

Cherry Hill

East 72nd Street

72nd Street Transverse

Rumsey
Playfield

East
Green

East 71st Street

Strawberry
Fields

Naumburg
Bandshell

Frick
Collection

East 70th Street

Asia Society
and Museum

East 69th Street

Sheep Meadow

East 68th Street

Hunter
College

68th Street
Hunter
College

East 67th Street

Central Park

Tisch
Children's
Zoo

East 66th Street

Tavern on
the Green

East 65th Street

65th Street Transverse

East 64th Street

Heckscher
Ballfields

Dairy Visitor
Center

Central Park
Zoo

East 63rd Street

Lexington Avenue/
63rd Street

Wollman
Skating Rink

East 62nd Street

250 m

East 61st Street

250 yds

West Drive

Central Park Drive

The Pond

East 60th Street

Lexington Avenue/
59th Street

5th Avenue/
59th Street

59th Street

Central Park South

East 59th Street

West 58th Street

East 58th Street

57th Street

WEST 57TH STREET

D

57th Street

Trump
Tower

E

EAST 57TH STREET

F

Carnegie
Hall

East 56th Street

CITY TOURS

105

Upper West Side Quick Reference Guide

American Museum of Natural History (▷ 14)

This is the largest natural history museum in the world. The life-size, rearing Barosaurus in the main entrance hall leads to the renowned dinosaur halls, where fossil specimens of some of the earliest dinosaur discoveries are displayed. Add to that a priceless collection of gemstones, animal displays, the Rose Center for Earth and Space with its amazing planetarium, and more, and you could easily spend a whole day here.

Lincoln Center (▷ 42)

New York's premier performing arts complex is a sight to behold, with its gushing fountains and gleaming buildings, the huge arched windows and chandeliers of the Metropolitan Opera House, and the glowing lights reflected in its wide central plaza. In addition to housing the Metropolitan Opera, it is home to the New York Philharmonic, the Juilliard School of Music, the New York City Ballet and many others, and offers a vast array of entertainment.

View of Central Park West, including the Dakota and San Remo apartment buildings

CITY TOURS

Farther Afield

New York's outer boroughs are predominantly residential, but there is still plenty to see, especially in Brooklyn (▷ 16–17). With an early start, you can take in its top sights as well as two classic New York experiences.

Morning
Join the morning bustle of the city's commuters and begin your day at the tip of Manhattan at the Staten Island Ferry Terminal. The ferry ride (right) across Upper New York Bay is stunning in both directions and it's free. If you can, ride on the ferry's outside deck to get a good view of the Statue of Liberty—visible from the right side of the boat on the outward journey—and other sights. The round trip to and from **Staten Island** (▷ 75) takes an hour; when you arrive you can catch the next ferry back to Manhattan. For a coffee and a late breakfast try The Gavel Grill, a block from the terminal at 9 Hyatt Street.

Mid-morning
Disembark and walk up Broadway to Bowling Green, where you can catch the No. 4 or 5 subway train to the Brooklyn Bridge/City Hall stop. On Park Row, a sidewalk entrance leads up to the wooden walkway of **Brooklyn Bridge** (left; ▷ 66). A walk (or jog) across the bridge is a must, and New Yorkers love it as much as visitors do. It's about a 20-minute walk, though it can take twice as long with stops to admire the views back to the Manhattan skyline.

Lunch
When you come to the end of the bridge, you'll have worked up an appetite so, when you see the DUMBO sign, take the stairwell down to the street and head toward the water. **Grimaldi's** (▷ 145) on Front Street has some of the best pizza in New York. Afterward, walk along the promenade for splendid vistas across the river to Manhattan.

Afternoon
Walk through the pretty brown-stone-lined streets of Brooklyn Heights to the Clark Street subway stop, and take No. 2 or 3 subway to the Eastern Parkway stop. This eastern side of Prospect Park contains two of Brooklyn's finest attractions: the **Brooklyn Museum** (right; ▷ 16–17) and **Brooklyn Botanic Garden** (990 Washington Avenue, tel 718/623-7200), with its rose garden, bonsai museum and Japanese Hill-and-Pond Garden. A visit to either could take up the afternoon.

Dinner
To get to Williamsburg and **Peter Luger Steak House** (▷ 148) for dinner, the quickest route is to take the No. 2 or 3 subway to Fulton Street in Manhattan and change to the J train to Marcy Avenue. If pricey red meat isn't your thing, stroll along Bedford Avenue, which is lined with inexpensive dining options.

Late evening
Williamsburg is filled with fun bars and live music. A good bet is the **Music Hall of Williamsburg** (66 N Sixth Street, tel 718/486-5400), which draws local talent, internationally known indie rockers, spoken word artists and more. Or venture into neighboring Greenpoint to the **Black Rabbit** (91 Greenpoint Avenue, tel 718/349-1595), a local watering hole with a friendly vibe.

Teaneck

Englewood

80

19

20

46 Saddle
Brook

Hackensack

17

4

Bogota

Garfield

80

95

Passaic

46

21

Hasbrouck
Heights

Ridgefield
Park

46

Palisades
Park

Fort
Lee

George
Washington
Bridge

PALISADES INTERSTATE

HENRY HUDSON PARKWAY

GARDEN STATE PARKWAY

3

Clifton

Wallington

17

Moonachie

Ridgefield

Fairview

125th

9

HARLEM

NEW
YORK

Nutley

3

Rutherford

NEW JERSEY

95

Hackensack River

Hudson River

Central
Park

Lyndhurst

95

9

West New
York

57th St

MANHATTAN

Belleville

North
Arlington

Secaucus

3

495 Weehawken

2nd Ave

Queensboro
Bridge

21

Kearny

NEW JERSEY TURNPIKE WESTERN SPUR

NEW JERSEY TURNPIKE EASTERN SPUR

Union
City

Lincoln
Tunnel

34th St

FDR DRIVE

East River

280

Harrison

280

1

Hoboken

9A

14th St

Newark

9

9

440

Jersey
City

78

Holland
Tunnel

78

Ellis
Island

Liberty
State
Park

Hugh L
Carey
Tunnel

Governors
Island

Brooklyn
Bridge

Manhattan
Bridge

278

1

9

95

Newark Liberty
International Airport

78

Statue
of Liberty

Brooklyn
Botanic
Garden

Prospect
Park

PROSPECT EXPY

27

440

Bayonne

Upper
New York
Bay

278

Newark
Bay

BOROUGH
PARK

278

OCEAN PARKWAY

NEW JERSEY TURNPIKE

440

Bayonne
Bridge

278

BELT PARKWAY

GRAVESEND

PORT
RICHMOND

CLIFTON

278

Verrazano
Narrows
Bridge

440

STATEN ISLAND

ARROCHAR

Lower
New York
Bay

Coney
Island

LIGHTHOUSE
HILL

LaTourette
Park

Gateway National
Recreation Area

GREAT
KILLS

WAKEFIELD

WOODSIDE

Van Cortlandt Park

Davids Island

Long Island Sound

New York Botanical Garden

The Cloisters

PELHAM GARDENS

Pelham Bay Park

Hart Island

SANDS POINT

Bronx Zoo

BRONX

City Island

Eastchester Bay

Yankee Stadium

KINGS POINT

HUNTS POINT

Bronx-Whitestone Bridge

Throgs Neck Bridge

Rikers Island

Robert F Kennedy Bridge

ASTORIA

LaGuardia Airport

NORTH HILLS

FLUSHING

ONG LAND CITY

GRAND CENTRAL PKWY

25A

Flushing Meadows-Corona Park

25A

QUEENS

ILLIAMSBURG

FOREST HILLS

GRAND CENTRAL PARKWAY

FLORAL PARK

EDFORD-UYVESANT

JACKIE ROBINSON PARKWAY

JAMAICA

NEW YORK

SOUTHERN STATE PARKWAY

ANTIC AVENUE

RICHMOND HILLS

VALLEY STREAM

ROOKLYN

EAST NEW YORK

EAST ATBUSH

CROSS BAY BOULEVARD

JFK International Airport

LAWRENCE

Gateway National Recreation Area

Floyd Bennett Field

FAR ROCKAWAY

Jamaica Bay

Atlantic Beach

Rockaway Beach

0   3 km

0   3 miles

Farther Afield Quick Reference Guide

⭐ SIGHTS AND EXPERIENCES

Brooklyn (▷ 16–17)
If you've ever wondered what New York is like beyond Manhattan, Brooklyn is the best place to start. Brooklyn Heights is lined with classic brownstones. The Brooklyn Museum contains a renowned Egyptian collection and the Sackler Center for Feminist Art. Alongside is the Brooklyn Botanic Garden. Walk back to Manhattan across the Brooklyn Bridge—a classic New York experience. Williamsburg, with its chic boutiques and bars, is lively on evenings and weekends.

MORE TO SEE	64

Bronx Zoo
The Cloisters
Coney Island
Flushing Meadows–Corona Park

Harlem
New York Botanical Garden
Staten Island
Yankee Stadium

SHOP	114

Vintage Clothing
Beacon's Closet

ENTERTAINMENT	126

Bars
Barbès
Union Hall

Live Music
Brooklyn Steel

EAT	138

Casual
Grimaldi's
Classic NY
Peter Luger Steak House

Contemporary
Blue Ribbon Brasserie
Henry's End
Fine Dining
River Café

CITY TOURS

Shop

Whether you're looking for the best local products, a department store or a quirky boutique, you'll find them all in New York. In this section shops are listed alphabetically.

SHOP

Introduction

Thought there was nothing you couldn't buy over the internet? Think again. New York is a shopping heaven, with clothing, furniture, food and souvenirs available no place else. Shopping is still one of the best ways to get an inside look at life in New York—its trends, pace, cultural influences and sense of humor. From massive department stores to small boutiques, the city has something for everyone.

One of a Kind

New York has seen a boom in artisanal and unique producers in the last decade, from chocolatiers to distilleries to jewelers. Keep an eye out for trunk shows, pop-up stores, and craft fairs where makers sell their wares.

Fashion

For fashion head for Nolita and SoHo, where small (and often expensive) boutiques line the streets. Major franchises can also be found here, along Broadway, and side streets such as Prince Street, Broome Street and Spring Street. For upscale fashion choices, head to Madison Avenue, north of 59th Street and 57th Street between 5th and Madison, where the smartest New York shops have outposts.

Music

Although the growth of downloads has seen the demise of many of the large music

WINDOW SHOPPING

Start on Lexington between 59th and 60th streets and you'll see the flags outside Bloomingdale's. Walk west to Madison Avenue; between 60th and 61st streets is Barney's, for expensive clothing, jewelry, accessories and beauty products. Walk west along 57th Street, past Chanel and Christian Dior, to Bergdorf Goodman. On Fifth Avenue peer in at Gucci, Tiffany's and Armani.

Clockwise from top: a store on Fifth Avenue; a T-shirt that says it all; pretzels to go; looking for a bargain at

retailers, there is still much to delight the enthusiast. The city's branches of Academy Records boast collections of vintage classical and rock vinyl and used CDs; Mercer Street Books and House of Oldies are prime browsing spots in Greenwich Village; or check out the Met Opera Shop at Lincoln Center for something a little more classical. Note that most American DVDs cannot be played on European machines.

Bargains

If you're looking for a bargain, try sample sales, where designer brands are marked down as much as 80 percent. Designer sales are often held at open showrooms over a few days. Arrive early on the first day of the sale for the best selection, though prices do drop as days go by. To find out about upcoming sales, visit thestylishcity.com/sample-sales-calendar.

A Bite to Eat

NYC is known for noshing: hot dogs, a slice of pizza, a bagel with a schmear or street food from mobile food vendors. These range from Middle Eastern falafel carts to waffle stands and spicy Korean and vegan lunch trucks. A handy guide to locating a gourmet food truck around town is roaminghunger.com.

SHOP

FLEA MARKETS

You can find everything from silver and beaded jewelry to clothing, collectibles, food, artworks and antiques at the Brooklyn Flea (brooklynflea.com), on Saturday in Industry City and on Sunday in DUMBO. Uptown, check out the huge GreenFlea market in Manhattan on Sunday, 10–5.30 (✉ Columbus Avenue between 76th and 77th streets 🕐 10–5.30). In good weather, weekend street fairs pop up in different neighborhoods. Check newyorkled.com/nyc_events_street_fairs.htm for a comprehensive list.

the Brooklyn Flea; don't miss the Midtown department stores; a boutique in Greenwich Village

Directory

LOWER MANHATTAN
Books
The Mysterious Bookshop
Clothes
Abercrombie & Fitch
Resurrection
Discount
Century 21
Food and Wine
The Pickle Guys
Homewares
New Kam Man

DOWNTOWN AND CHELSEA
Accessories
Village Tannery
Beauty
C.O. Bigelow
Kiehl's
Books
Barnes & Noble
Strand
Clothes
Cynthia Rowley
Hotoveli
Jeffrey New York
Kenneth Cole
Marc Jacobs
Food and Wine
Chelsea Market
Eataly
Union Square Greenmarket
Homewares
ABC Carpet and Home
Flying Tiger Copenhagen
Shoes
DSW
Toys
Kidding Around

MIDTOWN
Clothes
Brooks Brothers
Dolce & Gabbana
Thomas Pink
Department Stores
Bergdorf Goodman
Macy's
Saks Fifth Avenue
Shoes
Manolo Blahnik
Sports Goods
Niketown New York
Technology
Apple Store

UPPER EAST SIDE AND CENTRAL PARK
Books
Kitchen Arts and Letters
Clothes
Calvin Klein
Ralph Lauren
Department Stores
Barneys
Bloomingdale's

UPPER WEST SIDE
Accessories
Magpie
Beauty
Bluemercury Apothecary & Spa
Clothes
Malia Mills
Steven Alan
Food and Wine
Zabar's
Sports Goods
Patagonia

FARTHER AFIELD
Vintage Clothing
Beacon's Closet

Shopping A–Z

ABC CARPET AND HOME
abchome.com
Here are seven floors of extremely carefully edited homewares, from four-poster beds and handkerchiefs to artisanal lotions. The shared esthetic mixes mid-19th-century design museum, Venetian palace and deluxe hotel.
🔲 E15　✉ 888 Broadway/E 19th Street
☎ 212/473-3000　🚇 4, 5, 6, L, N, Q, R, W 14th Street–Union Square

ABERCROMBIE & FITCH
abercrombie.com
Teens and college grads are the core customers at this temple to slouchy American style, famous for its rather racy Bruce Weber-shot catalogs. The clothes for both men and women, though, are perfect for anyone's weekends and the prices are gentle.
🔲 F21　✉ 199 Water Street/Fulton Street
☎ 212/809-0789　(also 720 5th Avenue, tel 212/381-0110)　🚇 2, 3, 4, 5, A, C, J, Z Fulton Street–Broadway–Nassau

APPLE STORE
apple.com
This flagship store is certain to delight ingrained Mac-geeks as well as those in thrall to Apple's industry-leading design. Recently doubled in size, the store is always crowded with fans. Stores can also be found in the Meatpacking District, SoHo and the Upper East and West Sides.
🔲 E9　✉ 767 5th Avenue/59th Street
☎ 212/336-1440　🚇 N, R, W 5th Avenue–59th Street

BARNES & NOBLE
barnesandnoble.com
The flagship B&N has the widest new book selection in the city. Check the website for upcoming evening readings and regular book-signing events here and at several other locations.
🔲 E15　✉ 33 E 17th Street　☎ 212/253-0810　🚇 4, 5, 6, L, N, Q, R, W 14th Street–Union Square

BARNEYS
barneys.com
Some New Yorkers source their entire wardrobe from this high-fashion store. Ranging over several floors are avant-garde designers, the store's own-label clothes, high-end cosmetics, great menswear, an epic shoe department, jewelry,

The ABC Carpet and Home store

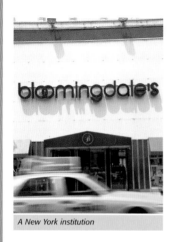
A New York institution

homewares, kids' clothes and more. The prices are high.

🔡 E9 ✉ 660 Madison Avenue/61st Street ☎ 212/826-8900 🚇 N, R, W 5th Avenue–59th Street

BEACON'S CLOSET

beaconscloset.com
This is one of the best vintage stores in Brooklyn's trendy Park Slope, with good-quality second-hand women's and men's clothing and shoes.

🔡 Off map ✉ 92 5th Avenue, Brooklyn ☎ 718/230-1630 🚇 Bergen Street

BERGDORF GOODMAN

bergdorfgoodman.com
For the most refined shopping experience, this eight-floor land-mark department store on the site of a Vanderbilt mansion takes the cake. The men's store is located right across the street.

🔡 E9 ✉ 754 5th Avenue/58th Street ☎ 212/753-7300 🚇 N, R, W 5th Avenue–59th Street

BLOOMINGDALE'S

bloomingdales.com
Bloomingdale's opened in 1879 and is one of the most venerable names in Manhattan, yet it keeps up with the latest trends. It's great for jewelry and handbags.

🔡 F9 ✉ Lexington/59th Street ☎ 212/705-2000 🚇 4, 5, 6, 9, F 43rd Street, 59th Street

BLUEMERCURY APOTHECARY & SPA

bluemercury.com
From top-brand cosmetics to spa treatments, hair care, fra-grances and candles, Bluemercury is a welcome addition to the Upper West Side retail experience.

🔡 B5 ✉ 2305 Broadway/83rd Street ☎ 212/799-0500 🚇 1 86th Street

BROOKS BROTHERS

brooksbrothers.com
Home of preppy fashions, Brooks Brothers caters to men, women and kids with everything from classic suits to sportswear. Their basics, like boxer shorts and white dress shirts, are exceptional.

🔡 E11 ✉ 346 Madison Avenue/44th Street ☎ 212/682-8800 🚇 4, 5, 6, 7, S Grand Central

---

THE SHOPS AT COLUMBUS CIRCLE

The closest thing to a mall in Manhattan, The Shops at Columbus Circle in the Time Warner Center has reclaimed Columbus Circle from the traffic. The stores are on the lowest four levels (restaurants above). The *pièce de résistance* is the Whole Foods Market, with a café. 🔡 C9 ✉ Time Warner Center, Broadway (59th/60th streets) ☎ 212/823-6300, shopsatcolumbuscircle.com 🚇 A, B, C, D, 1 59th Street–Columbus Circle

CALVIN KLEIN
calvinklein.com

The iconic New York designer's flagship store has enjoyed a recent makeover, with an Instagram-friendly deep gold interior and floor-to-ceiling beams—an art installation in itself. Check out the homeware and vintage quilts.

⊞ E9 ✉ 654 Madison Avenue/60th Street ☎ 212/292-9000 🚇 N, R, W 5th Avenue–59th Street

CENTURY 21
c21stores.com

Practically a cult, Century 21 sells discounted chic womenswear, especially by European designers. An uptown location can be found near Lincoln Center.

⊞ E21 ✉ 22 Cortlandt Street between Church Street and Broadway ☎ 212/227-9092 🚇 4, 5 Fulton Street

CHELSEA MARKET
chelseamarket.com

More than a store, this enormous former Nabisco factory has an array of independent food boutiques, bakeries, cafés, coffee shops and delis under one roof. Even if you're not hungry, it's enjoyable to stroll through for the architect-honed warehouse and inhale the mouthwatering aromas.

⊞ C15 ✉ 75 9th Avenue/15th Street ☎ 212/652-2110 🚇 A, C, E, L 14th Street

C.O. BIGELOW
bigelowchemists.com

The oldest apothecary in America (est. 1838) offers a wide range of products for pampering from head to toe. In addition to well-known international brands, the store also has its own line, with everything from lotions to natural remedies.

⊞ D16 ✉ 414 6th Avenue/9th Street ☎ 212/533-2700 🚇 A, B, C, D, E, F, M West 4th Street

CYNTHIA ROWLEY
cynthiarowley.com

Shop here for chic dresses, separates and shoes. There's also a sports and swimwear collection—check out the striking wetsuits.

⊞ C16 ✉ 394 Bleecker Street (between Perry and West 11th streets) ☎ 212/242-3803 🚇 1 Christopher Street–Sheridan Square

DOLCE & GABBANA
dolcegabbana.com

This is the flagship New York store for luxury cutting-edge styles from fashion's dynamic duo.

⊞ E9 ✉ 717 5th Avenue/55th Street ☎ 212/897-9653 🚇 N, R, W 5th Avenue E, M 5th Avenue–53rd Street

DSW
dsw.com

DSW stands for "Designer Shoe Warehouse," with Prada, Kate Spade, Via Spiga and other designer names at discounted prices. Choose from women's heels and pumps; men's loafers and sneakers; children's sandals and snowboots; handbags and more. Other branches in Midtown and the Upper West Side.

⊞ E15 ✉ 40 E 14th Street, Union Square South at University Place ☎ 212/674-2146 🚇 4, 5, 6, L, N, Q, R, W Union Square

EATALY
eataly.com/nyc

Offering a cornucopia of fresh and packaged Italian foodstuffs from coffee to gelato to homemade pastas, Eataly is as close as one can come to a real Italian food bazaar. There are also a dozen places to snack or dine.

🔲 D14 ✉ 200 5th Avenue/23rd Street
☎ 212/229-2560 🚇 6, R, W 23rd Street

FLYING TIGER COPENHAGEN

us.flyingtiger.com

The original US branch of this Danish chain is the go-to spot for whimsical gifts, toys and homeware at budget prices. Selections change seasonally—and are different in the US than in Europe—so every visit is a new experience.

🔲 E15 ✉ 920 Broadway/21st Street
☎ 212/777-1239 🚇 R, W 23rd Street

HOTOVELI

hotoveli.com

Chic French and Italian creations dominate in this edgy West Village clothing emporium. Think neutral tones, and well-made staples.

🔲 C16 ✉ 271 W 4th Street, between Perry and W 11th streets ☎ 212/206-7722
🚇 1 Christopher Street–Sheridan Square

JEFFREY NEW YORK

jeffreynewyork.com

One of the most fashionable places in the Meatpacking District, this compact designer store is the epitome of cool, with a DJ and an all-white interior. It all makes for a pleasant, but expensive, visit.

🔲 B15 ✉ 449 W 14th Street/9th–10th avenues ☎ 212/206-1272 🚇 A, C, E, L 14th Street

KENNETH COLE

kennethcole.com

Don't be fooled by the minimalist design of the clothier's flagship store: If what you are looking for isn't on display, the shop's high-tech digital touchscreens showcase the full line and the store will deliver same-day in the city.

🔲 F17 ✉ 328 Bowery/Bond Street
☎ 212/777-2013 🚇 6 Bleecker Street

KIDDING AROUND

kiddingaroundtoys.com

From newborns to teens, everyone will find something to their taste at this toy emporium, which stocks everything from board games to musical instruments. A branch is located in Grand Central Terminal.

🔲 E15 ✉ 60 W 15th Street/Avenue of the Americas ☎ 212/645-6337 🚇 F, M 14th Street; L 6th Avenue

KIEHL'S

kiehls.com

High-end face and body products for men and women. Made from naturally derived ingredients, the products are sold in upscale black-and-white packaging. The store has been an East Village fixture since 1851—the pear tree out front commemorates one that was planted by Dutch colonial governor Peter Stuyvesant.

🔲 F15 ✉ 109 3rd Avenue/13th Street
☎ 212/677-3171 🚇 L 3rd Avenue

SHOP

SINGULAR SOUVENIRS

Anyone can bring home an "I Love NY" T-shirt, but for more upscale gifts, try museum gift shops. The Metropolitan Museum (▷ 44–45) and MoMA (▷ 46–47) are well stocked, the American Folk Art Museum (▷ 66) has original offerings, and the Tenement Museum (▷ 72–73) on the Lower East Side has the best selection of NYC-themed books. Prefer to eat? The Pickle Guys (▷ 124) ships across the USA. Or check out the New York City Transit Museum shop at Grand Central Terminal for unique gifts—subway token watches, anyone?

KITCHEN ARTS AND LETTERS

kitchenartsandletters.com

This independent bookstore specializing in food and drink stocks the latest bestsellers, as well as classics from leading chefs such as James Beard and Julia Child. The helpful staff can also source rare and out-of-print titles for you.

➕ E4 ✉ 1435 Lexington Avenue, between 93rd and 94th streets ☎ 212/876-5550 🚇 6 96th Street

MACY'S

macys.com

The sign outside says it's the largest store in the world, and by the time you've explored all 11 levels of this huge department store, you'll believe it.

➕ D12 ✉ 151 W 34th Street/Herald Square ☎ 212/695-4400 🚇 1, 2, 3, B, D, F, M, N, Q, R 34th Street

MAGPIE

magpienewyork.com

This charming Upper West Side boutique is a treasure trove of goodies. It has everything from jewelry to baby clothes to food, all with an eco-friendly vibe.

➕ B5 ✉ 488 Amsterdam Avenue/84th Street ☎ 212/579-3003 🚇 1 86th Street

MALIA MILLS

maliamills.com

This swimwear emporium is cherished by every woman who fears her reflection. There are mix-and-match pieces made to fit all sizes and shapes, in stylish designs. There's also a line of versatile everyday clothing.

➕ C7 ✉ 220 Columbus Avenue/70th Street ☎ 212/874-7200 🚇 1, 2, 3 72nd Street

MANOLO BLAHNIK

manoloblahnik.com

Come here for beautifully made, extravagant shoes by one of the world's great shoe designers.

➕ D10 ✉ 31 W 54th Street ☎ 212/582-3007 🚇 E, M 5th Avenue–53rd Street

MARC JACOBS

marcjacobs.com

Fashion's favorite darling, Marc Jacobs put once-Bohemian Bleecker Street on the retail map.

➕ C16 ✉ 400 Bleecker Street/ W 11th Street ☎ 212/620-4021 🚇 1 Christopher Street–Sheridan Square

The largest store in the world

SHOP

THE MYSTERIOUS BOOKSHOP

mysteriousbookshop.com

This is a must for crime and mystery lovers. Staff will lead you to new discoveries alongside writers such as Patricia Highsmith and Raymond Chandler. Rare books are available.

➕ E20 ✉ 58 Warren Street between Church Street and West Broadway ☎ 212/587-1011 🚇 1, 2, 3, A, C, E Chambers Street

NEW KAM MAN

This Chinatown shop calls itself a "destination for all things Asian," and it's easy to see why. From home decor to herbal remedies, kitchenware to take-out food, there's a bit of everything here to please everyone.

➕ F19 ✉ 200 Canal Street/Mulberry Street ☎ 212/571-0330 🚇 6, J, N, Q, R, W, Z Canal Street

NIKETOWN

nike.com

This lavish SoHo newcomer has everything in sportswear, plus high-tech videos and trial zones

The Mysterious Bookshop

to test equipment. A 5th Avenue store is in the works.

➕ E18 ✉ 529 Broadway ☎ 646/716-3740 🚇 6 Spring Street; R, W Prince Street

PATAGONIA

patagonia.com

If you like environmental consciousness with your outdoor wear but still want to look slick while climbing a mountain or skiing, or just look like you might have done so, this is your place.

➕ C6 ✉ 426 Columbus Avenue/81st Street ☎ 917/441-0011 🚇 B, C 81st Street–Museum of Natural History

THE PICKLE GUYS

thepickleguys.com

The Pickle Guys still brine the old-fashioned way, selling pickles, olives, pickled watermelon (in season) and more out of barrels in their small storefront, much as it might have been done a century ago.

➕ G19 ✉ 357 Grand Street/Essex Street ☎ 212/656-9739 🚇 F Delancey Street; J, Z Essex Street

RALPH LAUREN

ralphlauren.com

Distinguished cowboy and English country heritage looks are sold at the Rhinelander Mansion, a beautiful turn-of-the-century house.

➕ E7 ✉ 867 Madison Avenue, between E 71st and 72nd streets ☎ 212/606-2100 🚇 6 68th Street–Hunter College

RESURRECTION

resurrectionvintage.com

You'll find a haul of pricey but perfect vintage, with an emphasis on collectible labels, including Halston, Courrèges and Ossie

Clarke. The owners offer their own line of skirts and tops.

F18 ✉ 45 Great Jones Street/ E Third Street ☎ 212/625-1374 🚇 6 Astor Place

SAKS FIFTH AVENUE
saksfifthavenue.com
Found on the famous street with the same name, this is Saks' flagship store. It stocks a fabulous range of luxury designer fashions.

E10 ✉ 611 5th Avenue/49th–50th streets ☎ 212/753-4000 🚇 E, F 5th Avenue

STEVEN ALAN
stevenalan.com
A Lower East Side look on the Upper West Side, this is a carefully edited array of cutting-edge labels, some of them available nowhere else—including Alan's own designs.

B5 ✉ 465 Amsterdam Avenue/82nd Street ☎ 212/595-8451 (also at 103 Franklin Street, 212/343-0692) 🚇 1, 2, 3 79th Street–Broadway; A, C, E 81st Street–Central Park West

STRAND
strandbooks.com
Filled with 18 miles (29km) of new, used and rare books, this fabulous bookstore is a New York City institution. It sells anything, from popular and hot-off-the-press bestsellers to antique volumes bought from estate sales. The New York City section is particularly strong.

E16 ✉ 828 Broadway/12th Street ☎ 212/473-1452 🚇 4, 5, 6, L, N, Q, R, W Union Square

THOMAS PINK
thomaspink.com
Beautifully tailored shirts for men and women line the shelves of the New York outlet of this classic

GREAT GREENMARKET
On four days a week (🕐 Mon, Wed, Fri, Sat 8–6) Union Square is home to the city's biggest and best greenmarket (grownyc.org/greenmarket). An entire culture has grown around this collection of stalls overflowing with homegrown and homemade produce from farms in the tri-state area. Favorites include maple candies, Amish cheeses and New York honey from rooftop beehives.

British label. Quality ties, socks and belts are also available.

E10 ✉ 520 Madison Avenue/E 53rd Street ☎ 212/838-1928 🚇 E, M 5th Avenue–53rd Street

VILLAGE TANNERY
villagetannery.com
Love leather? Look no further—stylish leather goods, designed by artisan Sevestet, are made to order and handcrafted from the finest materials. Choose from handbags, briefcases, totes, backpacks, belts and more.

D17 ✉ 173 Bleecker Street ☎ 212/673-5444 🚇 A, B, C, D, E, F, M West 4th Street–Washington Square

ZABAR'S
zabars.com
This gourmet foodie emporium has a Jewish soul all its own and is still going strong after 80 years. Cheese, coffee, smoked fish, caviar, bread, bagels and the like are on sale downstairs, while upstairs showcases the city's best buys in kitchenwares and housewares. There's an on-site café if you can't wait to sample the produce.

B6 ✉ 2245 Broadway/80th Street ☎ 212/787-2000 🚇 1 79th Street

SHOP

Entertainment

Once you're done with sightseeing for the day, you'll find lots of other great things to do with your time in this chapter, even if all you want to do is relax with a drink. In this section, establishments are listed alphabetically.

ENTERTAINMENT

Introduction

As the sun sets over New York, the city becomes a sultry, romantic and mysterious place. For spectacular sunset views, stroll along the pedestrian path on the banks of the Hudson River on the West Side, then wander through Times Square as the bright billboards pop out from the dark sky.

Nightlife

As young New Yorkers explore new frontiers in the city, the Meatpacking District—once known for drugs and prostitution—has become home to bars and clubs. You never know who might show at the chic Top of the Standard (848 Washington Street, tel 212/645-7600) and Cielo (18 Little West 12th Street, tel 646/543-8556). At the other end of the spectrum are neighborhood joints such as the Ear Inn (326 Spring Street at Washington Street, tel 212/226-9060) and Fat Cat (75 Christopher Street in West Village, tel 212/675-6056)—friendly dives where the beer flows cheaply and the music is loud.

A short stroll away, a string of music bars sit cheek by jowl along two blocks of Bleecker Street between LaGuardia Place and Sullivan Street, including the classic folk-rock haven The Bitter End (147 Bleecker Street, tel 212/673-7030), still going strong after more than 50 years. Around the corner is Café Wha? (▷ 132), where Dylan and Hendrix once played, and now a nightclub.

FOR A LAUGH

Comedy clubs are a great way to sample New York's sense of humor. Venues such as Caroline's on Broadway (✉ 1626 Broadway, at 50th Street ☎ 212/757-4100, carolines.com), Upright Citizens Brigade Theatre (✉ 555 W 42nd Street/11th Avenue ☎ 212/366-9176; also 153 E 3rd Street/Avenue A ☎ 212/366-9231, ucbtheatre.com), Stand Up NY (▷ 137) and Gotham (▷ 134) are popular.

Clockwise from top: Blue Note in Greenwich Village is one of the best places for jazz; the old Paramount Theater, Times Square; Alice Tully Hall, Lincoln Center;

Another hot nightlife neighborhood is the Lower East Side, where there's a multitude of bars fanning out from Ludlow and Stanton streets. Leading the pack are Arlene's Grocery (▷ 131), Pianos (158 Ludlow Street, tel 212/505-3733) and Rockwood Music Hall (196 Allen Street, tel 212/477-4155).

Broadway and Beyond
Top Broadway shows can be expensive, but you can pick up some great bargains at the TKTS booth in Times Square and other locations (tdf.org/tkts). Off-Broadway venues are less expensive and you might catch the next big hit on its way up. A night at Lincoln Center (▷ 42–43) is an unforgettable New York experience, whether you opt for a production at the Metropolitan Opera (▷ 135), a symphony at David Geffen Hall (▷ 133), a ballet at the David H. Koch Theater (▷ 133), or one of the more intimate venues.

Take to the Water
Circle Line Cruises' evening boat rides around Manhattan are a relaxing and memorable way to experience the world's most famous skyline. Board at Pier 83, at 42nd Street on the Hudson River (tel 212/563-3200). Tour guides on board relate the legends of the city (circleline42.com).

LIVE MUSIC

Rock bands perform at Bowery Ballroom (✉ 6 Delancey Street ☎ 212/260-4700, boweryballroom.com) and Irving Plaza (✉ 17 Irving Plaza ☎ 212/777-6800, irving-plaza.com). Madison Square Garden (▷ 134) hosts blockbuster tours. There's everything from classical music to pop at Carnegie Hall (▷ 132). Among the top jazz clubs are Blue Note (▷ 132) and Village Vanguard (✉ 178 7th Avenue South ☎ 212/255-4037, villagevanguard.com) in Greenwich Village, and Iridium in Midtown (✉ 1650 Broadway ☎ 212/582-2121, theiridium.com).

Gotham Comedy Club; a quiet table à deux in the Meatpacking District; take to the water to see the New York skyline by night

Directory

LOWER MANHATTAN
Bars
The Dead Rabbit Grocery and Grog
Parkside Lounge
The Porterhouse at Fraunces Tavern
Wassail
Cinema
Film Forum
Clubs
Arlene's Grocery
SOB's
Comedy
Comedy Cellar
Live Music
City Winery

DOWNTOWN AND CHELSEA
Bars
McSorley's Old Ale House
Pete's Tavern
White Horse Tavern
Cabaret
Duplex (▷ panel, 134)
Joe's Pub
Clubs
Café Wha?
Comedy
Gotham Comedy Club
Jazz
Blue Note
Live Music
Mercury Lounge
Theater/Performance
Cherry Lane Theatre

MIDTOWN
Bars
Four Seasons Hotel TY Bar
Classical Music
Carnegie Hall
Jazz
Birdland
Live Music
Madison Square Garden
PlayStation Theater
Theater/Performance
The New Victory Theater

New World Stages
Radio City Music Hall
Signature Theatre
TV Show Recording
The Tonight Show starring Jimmy
   Fallon

UPPER EAST SIDE AND CENTRAL PARK
Bars
Auction House
Comedy
Dangerfield's
Jazz
Café Carlyle
Literary Events/Readings
92nd Street Y
Theater/Performance
Florence Gould Hall
Shakespeare in the Park

UPPER WEST SIDE
Bars
Ascent
Classical Music
Cathedral of St. John the Divine
David Geffen Hall
Metropolitan Opera
Comedy
Stand Up NY
Dance
David H. Koch Theater
Jazz
Dizzy's Club Coca Cola
Smoke
Live Music
Beacon Theatre
Theater/Performance
Symphony Space

FARTHER AFIELD
Bars
Barbès
Union Hall
Live Music
Brooklyn Steel

Entertainment A–Z

92ND STREET Y
92Y.org
A varied program of events is held here, including readings by renowned authors, folk music, jazz and lectures on a range of subjects.
➕ E4 ✉ 1395 Lexington Avenue/92nd Street ☎ 212/415-5500 🚇 6 96th Street

ARLENE'S GROCERY
arlenesgrocery.net
This is one of the best live music clubs in the city. Arlene's prides itself on helping new bands.
➕ G18 ✉ 95 Stanton Street, between Ludlow and Orchard streets ☎ 212/358-1633 🚇 F, M 2nd Avenue

ASCENT
ascentloungenyc.com
Enjoy impressively designed surroundings, fine food and drink, and stunning views of Central Park and Broadway at this elegant bar.
➕ C9 ✉ Time Warner Center, Columbus Circle ☎ 212/823-9770 🚇 A, B, C, D 59th Street–Columbus Circle

AUCTION HOUSE
theauctionhousenyc.com
With sumptuous red velvet drapes, a fireplace, sofas and candlelight, this is more suited to a romantic drink than a rowdy night out. The no-furs, no-sneakers dress code gives an idea of the casual-chic ambience.
➕ F4 ✉ 300 E 89th Street/2nd Avenue ☎ 212/427-4458 🚇 Q 86th Street

Check out the cocktails

BARBÈS
barbesbrooklyn.com
This Brooklyn bar and live music venue is named after a neighborhood in Paris known for its North African community. In its intimate performance space at the back, Barbès stages an eclectic music program, from Slavic soul to Afrobeat and Cuban jazz.
➕ Off map ✉ 376 9th Street ☎ 347/422-0248 🚇 F 7th Avenue

BEACON THEATRE
beacontheatre.com
The Beacon is one of the premier venues in the city, featuring multi-night stands by legendary artists such as Bob Dylan and Ringo Starr, as well as many rising stars.
➕ B7 ✉ 2124 Broadway/74th Street ☎ 212/465-6500 🚇 1, 2, 3 72nd Street

COCKTAIL CULTURE

Cocktail culture is alive and well in the Big Apple. The Martini craze is here to stay—many lounges and bars offer long menus of creative concoctions. Elegant glassware is crucial. Atmospheres range from urban chic to clubby lounge to bars. Rooftop bars with a view are very popular. Neighborhood pubs, with more emphasis on beer and bourbon, are favorite watering holes.

ENTERTAINMENT

Carnegie Hall

BIRDLAND

birdlandjazz.com

Big names, big bands, John Coltrane tributes and Cubans are the rage here. The club was established here in 1949.

⊞ C11 ✉ 315 W 44th Street/8th–9th avenues ☎ 212/581-3080 🚇 A, C, E 42nd Street–Port Authority Bus Terminal

BLUE NOTE

bluenote.net

Jazz artists play two shows nightly at this popular Village club and restaurant. The Sunday brunch deal of food and a show is great value.

⊞ D17 ✉ 131 W 3rd Street/6th Avenue–MacDougal Street ☎ 212/475-8592 🚇 A, B, C, D, E, F, M 4th Street–Washington Square

BROOKLYN STEEL

bowerypresents.com

This new music venue in happening Williamsburg is a huge, down-to-earth, 1,800-capacity space, favoring indie-rock bands, plus major DJ sets.

⊞ Off map ✉ 319 Frost Street ☎ 888/929-7849 🚇 L Graham Avenue

CAFÉ CARLYLE

thecarlyle.com

This lounge in the Carlyle Hotel is home to smooth singers and jazz bands. Look in at Bemelmans Bar, with its murals of Central Park by Ludwig Bemelmans.

⊞ E6 ✉ 35 E 76th Street, Madison Avenue ☎ 212/744-1600 🚇 6 77th Street

CAFÉ WHA?

cafewha.com

In business since the 1950s, this has been a hot spot ever since Bob Dylan and Jimi Hendrix used to hang out here. Bruce Springsteen started his career here. It's still going strong, with bands performing nightly and styles ranging from R&B to soul, modern rock and indie pop.

⊞ D17 ✉ 115 MacDougal Street/Minetta Lane ☎ 212/254-3706 🚇 A, B, C, D, E, F, M 4th Street–Washington Square

CARNEGIE HALL

carnegiehall.org

This world-class venue, which houses three recital halls, features an eclectic program from classical artists to folk singers, world music and pop. With so much choice, there's something for everyone.

⊞ D9 ✉ 881 7th Avenue/57th Street ☎ 212/247-7800 🚇 N, Q, R, W 57th Street; E 7th Avenue

CATHEDRAL OF ST. JOHN THE DIVINE

stjohndivine.org

The cathedral provides a varied program of liturgical, cultural and civic events including choral, classical and poetry recitals.

⊞ B1 ✉ 1047 Amsterdam Avenue/112th Street ☎ 212/316-7540 🚇 1 Cathedral Parkway–110th Street

CHERRY LANE THEATRE

cherrylanetheatre.org

This historic theater in Greenwich Village presents a vibrant program of landmark plays and works by emerging playwrights.

➕ C17 ✉ 38 Commerce Street between Barrow and Bedford streets ☎ 866/811-4111 🚇 1 Christopher Street–Sheridan Square

CITY WINERY

citywinery.com/newyork

Events at the City Winery range from intimate evenings with singer-songwriters to gourmet cooking demonstrations. It's also a fully functioning winery, with tastings and a shop.

➕ D18 ✉ 155 Varick Street/Vandam Street ☎ 212/608-0555 🚇 C, E Spring Street; 1 Houston

COMEDY CELLAR

comedycellar.com

A cozy Greenwich Village spot, this attracts well-known comedians from time to time. The intimate nature of the venue means you are quite likely to find you are part of the show, so be warned.

➕ D17 ✉ 117 MacDougal Street, between W 3rd Street and Minetta Lane, and 130 W 3rd Street ☎ 212/254-3480 🚇 A, B, C, D, E, F, M 4th Street–Washington Square

DANGERFIELD'S

dangerfields.com

This basement comedy club, established in 1969, is still going strong and claims to be the oldest in the world. Those that have performed on its tiny stage include Jay Leno and Jim Carrey.

➕ F9 ✉ 1118 1st Avenue/61st Street ☎ 212/593-1650 🚇 4, 5, 6 59th Street

DAVID GEFFEN HALL

lincolncenter.org

In 2015, David Geffen donated $100 million to rename and revamp the Avery Fisher Hall concert venue. It's home to the New York Philharmonic, but touring artists and orchestras also come to perform here.

➕ B8 ✉ 10 Lincoln Center Plaza, Columbus Avenue/65th Street ☎ 212/875-5030 🚇 1 66th Street–Lincoln Center

DAVID H. KOCH THEATER

davidhkochtheater.com

nycballet.com

The sumptuous home of the New York City Ballet, which performs here September through June.

➕ B8 ✉ 20 Lincoln Center Plaza at 63rd Street ☎ 212/496-0600 🚇 1 66th Street–Lincoln Center

THE DEAD RABBIT GROCERY AND GROG

deadrabbitnyc.com

Every drink on the Dead Rabbit's extensive upstairs menu is historically sourced, giving patrons a flavor of old New York.

➕ E23 ✉ 30 Water Street/Broad Street ☎ 646/422-7906 🚇 1 South Ferry; R, W Whitehall

KEEPING UP

With so much happening in New York, it helps to have updated lists of what's on. Look for weekly listings in the *New York* and *The New Yorker* magazines, the Friday and Sunday editions of the *New York Times* or online at timeout.com. Free copies of the *New York Press* may be found in storefronts and vestibules around town. The monthly listings in *Paper* magazine have a decidedly downtown focus. nycgo.com is the city's tourism website.

DIZZY'S CLUB COCA COLA
jazz.org/dizzys
Jazz at Lincoln Circle's intimate club is—in the spirit of Dizzy Gillespie—designed to ensure that performers and spectators alike relaaaaax. There are late-night sessions Tuesday through Saturday.
C9 ✉ Time Warner Center at Broadway/60th Street, 5th floor
☎ 212/258-9595 🚇 1, A, B, C, D 59th Street–Columbus Circle

FILM FORUM
filmforum.com
New York's best revival house shows everything from silent films (with live accompaniment) to independent movie premieres, documentaries and classics.
D18 ✉ 209 W Houston Street/Varick Street ☎ 212/727-8110 🚇 1 Houston Street

FLORENCE GOULD HALL
fiaf.org
Associated with the Alliance Française, this concert hall stages music, dance, jazz and readings with a French theme.
E9 ✉ 55 E 59th Street/Park–Madison avenues ☎ 212/355-6160 🚇 N, R, W 5th Avenue–59th Street

FOUR SEASONS HOTEL TY BAR
fourseasons.com/newyork
I.M. Pei design, a smooth vibe and a great Martini menu make the TY lobby bar an excellent choice for cocktails.
E9 ✉ 57 E 57th Street/Madison Avenue
☎ 212/758-5700 🚇 4, 5, 6 Lexington Avenue–59th Street

GOTHAM COMEDY CLUB
gothamcomedyclub.com
Gotham showcases top stars (including the likes of Jerry Seinfeld, Larry David and Dave Chappelle), as well as up-and-coming comedians.
C14 ✉ 208 W 23rd Street/7th Avenue
☎ 212/367-9000 🚇 1 23rd Street; F, Path 23rd Street

JOE'S PUB
joespub.publictheater.org
Known for its sound quality, Joe's always has an interesting, varied line-up of singers, comedians, magicians and burlesque artists.
E16 ✉ The Public Theater, 425 Lafayette Street/Astor Place ☎ 212/539-8778 🚇 R, W 8th Street–NYU; 6 Astor Place

MADISON SQUARE GARDEN
thegarden.com
The giant concrete circle, often called MSG, is one of the city's major venues for music and sporting events. For the box office enter the Main Ticket Lobby at 7th Avenue and 32nd Street.
C13 ✉ 4 Pennsylvania Plaza
☎ 212/465-6741 🚇 1, 2, 3, A, C, E 34th Street–Penn Station

CABARET

The term has undergone so many image overhauls, it's now settled into being a catch-all for entertainment options ranging from off-Broadway cabaret theater and downtown crooners sitting around the piano bar at Duplex (✉ 61 Christopher Street ☎ 212/255-5438, theduplex.com) to the Broadway supper club at 54 Below (☎ 254 W 54th Street ☎ 646/476-3551, 54below.com). Joe's Pub (above) is among the venues that offer what you might call classic, though modernized, cabaret.

New York's late-night scene ranges from all-night parties to more staid amusements. The Meatpacking District is home to many popular spots, including sister clubs Le Bain (🏢 444 W 13th Street ☎ 212/645-7600), with its rooftop hot tubs, and Top of the Standard (🏢 848 Washington Street), atop the High Line. At the IFC Center (🏢 323 6th Avenue/W 3rd Street ☎ 212/924-7771), scary weekend Midnight Movies have a loyal following

MCSORLEY'S OLD ALE HOUSE

mcsorleysoldalehouse.nyc

New York's oldest saloon (1854) served Abe Lincoln and John Lennon, and still draws a crowd with its sawdust-covered floors, coal-burning stove and working-class history.

🏢 F16 ✉ 15 E 7th Street/3rd Avenue
☎ 212/473-9148 🚇 6 Astor Place

MERCURY LOUNGE

mercuryloungenyc.com

Its laid-back atmosphere attracts eclectic performers and tickets are very reasonable. The Strokes famously got their start here.

🏢 F17 ✉ 217 E Houston Street/Essex Street ☎ 212/260-4700 🚇 F 2nd Avenue

METROPOLITAN OPERA

metopera.org

The gala openings at this world-class opera house rank among the most glamorous of the city's events. Visit the website at noon for same-day rush tickets. The season runs from October to April.

🏢 B8 ✉ 30 Lincoln Center ☎ 212/362-6000 🚇 1 66th Street–Lincoln Center

THE NEW VICTORY THEATER

newvictory.org

If you have kids (five or older), there'll be something here to thrill them and keep them entertained.

🏢 C11 ✉ 209 W 42nd Street/7th–8th avenues ☎ 646/223-3010 🚇 1, 2, 3, 7, N, Q, R, S, W Times Square–42nd Street

NEW WORLD STAGES

newworldstages.com

Check out the top off-Broadway productions, from musicals to kids' shows, at this state-of-the-art theatrical venue.

🏢 C10 ✉ 340 W 50th Street/8th Avenue
☎ 646/871-1730 🚇 C, E 50th Street

PARKSIDE LOUNGE

parksidelounge.net

Parkside hosts live music, stand-up and karaoke, as well as people just having a beer. It's open until 4am.

🏢 G17 ✉ 317 E Houston Street/
Attorney Street ☎ 212/673-6270
🚇 F, M 2nd Avenue

PETE'S TAVERN

petestavern.com

A favorite with locals, this fine 150-year-old Gramercy Park saloon has a welcoming feel. The happy hour (Mon–Fri 4–7) serves free hors d'oeuvres.

SUMMER IN THE CITY

One of the best reasons to brave the summer heat in New York is for the wonderful choice of free entertainment put on by many of the city's premier cultural institutions. Without paying a dime it's possible to enjoy alfresco operas, theater, art, eating, jazz, classical music, movies, dance, rock-and-roll, blues and folk music. Many people arrive early for park performances by popular artists and stake out a good spot for a picnic.

ENTERTAINMENT

➕ E15 ✉ 129 E 18th Street/Irving Place
☎ 212/473-7676 🚇 4, 5, 6, L, N, Q, R, W
14th Street–Union Square

PLAYSTATION THEATER

playstationtheater.com

This theater is a medium-size venue for decent music acts in a great location in Times Square.

➕ C11/D11 ✉ 1515 Broadway/44th
Street ☎ 212/930-1950 🚇 1, 2, 3, 7, N, Q,
R, S, W Times Square–42nd Street

THE PORTERHOUSE AT FRAUNCES TAVERN

frauncestavern.com

This 18th-century watering hole is the first US branch of Dublin's Porterhouse Brewing Company. It has fine ales, live music and DJs.

➕ E22 ✉ 54 Pearl Street/Broad Street
☎ 212/968-1776 🚇 R, W Whitehall Street

Radio City, famous since the 1930s

RADIO CITY MUSIC HALL

radiocity.com

This landmark art deco theater hosts major music and family shows. The holiday show is a city tradition. One-hour tours offered.

➕ D10 ✉ 1260 6th Avenue/50th Street
☎ 212/247-4777 🕐 Varied; tours daily
9.30–5 🚇 B, D, F, M 40th–50th streets–
Rockefeller Center

SHAKESPEARE IN THE PARK

publictheater.org

The Shakespeare festival is a high-light of summer in Central Park. Line up for free tickets from noon on performance days, or chance your luck with virtual ticketing.

➕ C6 ✉ Delacorte Theater in Central Park,
81st Street (west side) ☎ 212/539-8500
🚇 B, C 81st Street

SIGNATURE THEATRE

signaturetheatre.org

Every season at this off-Broadway house, designed by Frank Gehry, has a new playwright-in-residence from the first ranks of American theater. Even without tickets, you can enjoy the café/bar.

➕ B11 ✉ 480 W 42nd Street/10th Avenue
☎ 212/244-7529 🚇 A, C, E 42nd Street

SMOKE

smokejazz.com

This intimate jazz lounge hosts both local and well-known names. The fixed-price dinners are good value, as is the Sunday brunch.

✚ B2 ✉ 2751 Broadway/106th Street
☎ 212/864-6662 ⓢ 1 103rd Street

SOB'S
sobs.com
The Latin beat keeps you dancing at the tropically themed nightclub, Sounds of Brazil. Hear African, reggae and other island music.
✚ D18 ✉ 204 Varick Street/Houston Street
☎ 212/243-4940 ⓢ 1 Houston Street

STAND UP NY
standupny.com
Aspiring comics try out their new routines in this traditional comedy club that has also hosted the likes of Jerry Seinfeld, Chris Rock and Jon Stewart.
✚ B6 ✉ 236 W 78th Street/Broadway
☎ 212/595-0850 ⓢ 1 79th Street

SYMPHONY SPACE
symphonyspace.org
Head here for storytelling, readings, children's theater, music, dance, film, poetry, comedy and more. There's often more than one show a day.
✚ B4 ✉ 2537 Broadway/95th Street
☎ 212/864-5400 ⓢ 1, 2, 3 96th Street

THE TONIGHT SHOW STARRING JIMMY FALLON
nbc.com/the-tonight-show
Upon taking the helm of *The Tonight Show*, Jimmy Fallon moved it back to New York City for the first time in decades. Take your chance at same-day standby tickets by lining up before 9am on 49th Street across from *The Today Show*.
✚ D10 ✉ 30 Rockefeller Plaza/49th Street
☎ 212/664-3056 ⓢ B, D, F, M 47th–50th Streets–Rockefeller Center

UNION HALL
unionhallny.com
This casual lounge-bar/restaurant in Brooklyn's Park Slope has two popular *bocce* lanes (like indoor bowls), outdoor garden seating and a basement stage for regular live music and comedy. It's open until 4am.
✚ Off map ✉ 702 Union Street/5th Avenue ☎ 718/638-4400 ⓢ Union Street

WASSAIL
wassailnyc.com
Home to 90-plus domestic and imported ciders on tap and in bottles, this bar has taken the Lower East Side by storm. It also serves seasonal vegetarian food.
✚ G18 ✉ 162 Orchard Street/Stanton Street ☎ 646/918-6835 ⓢ F 2nd Avenue

WHITE HORSE TAVERN
whitehorsetavern1880.com
This sprawling 1880s bar has been popular with writers and artists over the years, and was the last watering hole of Welsh poet Dylan Thomas. It serves bar food, including weekend brunch.
✚ C16 ✉ 567 Hudson Street/11th Street
☎ 212/989-3956 ⓢ 1 Christopher Street–Sheridan Square

ENTERTAINMENT

BIG IN NEW YORK
From the elegance of a grand opera to the excitement of avant-garde performance art, New York spectacles are world-class (even the flops). Broadway shows can be expensive, but nothing transports audiences like a great multimillion-dollar musical or an intense performance by a drama diva. Reserve tickets well in advance for the most popular shows.

Eat

**There are places to eat across the city to
suit all tastes and budgets. In this section
establishments are listed alphabetically.**

EAT

Introduction

In this global melting pot, you can find just about every world cuisine from African to Vietnamese in settings from budget hole-in-the wall to haute cuisine palaces.

New Takes on Tradition

New York also has its own dining traditions for visitors to share, with dishes like New York strip steaks and Manhattan clam chowder. But other favorites change with the times. Brunch is still the classic weekend ritual in Greenwich Village and SoHo, but healthier veggie choices are now in the mix (▷ 144). As the legendary New York delis are disappearing, updated versions like Russ and Daughters Café are taking their place (127 Orchard Street/Delancey-Rivington, tel 212-475-4880). Food halls with many choices are multiplying (▷ 142). Pizza by the slice remains a city standby. To sample the traditional thin-crusted New York pizza baked in a coal-fired, brick-oven, visit pioneers like Grimaldi's, in Brooklyn (▷ 145), or Johns, 302 E 12th street (tel 212/475-9531).

Fine Dining

You can enjoy world-class dining in New York, at places like Per Se (▷ 148), Le Bernardin (▷ 142) or Eleven Madison Park (▷ 144), but reserve well in advance. Top restaurants have top prices, close to $200 per person, including tax and tip.

TAXES, TIPPING AND FINANCIAL MATTERS

A sales tax of 8.875 percent will be added to your dining bill. The minimum tip (with good service) is 15 percent; people often double the tax for a 17.75 percent tip. Many restaurants offer fixed-price menus, which are good value. Watch for New York Restaurant Week, held twice a year in winter and summer. This special promotion offers a three-course menu at reduced rates for lunch and dinner at many restaurants; this deal is often extended so it's always worth checking if it's available.

From top: pancakes with maple syrup in a New York diner; the city has some great pizzerias; Café Boulud, a top restaurant; cheeseburger with fries

Directory

LOWER MANHATTAN
Asian
Mission Chinese Food
Oriental Garden
Casual
The Bailey
Bubby's
Delicatessen
Classic NY
Katz's Deli
The Odeon
Fine Dining
Delmonico's

DOWNTOWN AND CHELSEA
American
Union Square Café
Asian
Momofuku Ssäm Bar
Pondicheri
Contemporary
North Square
The Spotted Pig
Fine Dining
Del Posto
Eleven Madison Park
Gotham Bar and Grill
Ukrainian
Veselka

MIDTOWN
Asian
Kajitsu
Nobu Fifty Seven
Casual
Forty Carrots
Grand Central Terminal Dining
    Concourse (▷ panel, 145)
John's Pizzeria
Classic NY
'21' Club
Oyster Bar

Fine Dining
Le Bernardin
Casa Lever
Per Se
Greek
Uncle Nick's

UPPER EAST SIDE AND CENTRAL PARK
Casual
Jackson Hole
Classic NY
The Loeb Boathouse
Fine Dining
Daniel
French
Café Boulud
Middle Eastern
A La Turka
Persepolis

UPPER WEST SIDE
Casual
Barney Greengrass
Boat Basin Café
Fine Dining
Jean-Georges
Italian
Carmine's
Mexican
Rosa Mexicano
Vegetarian
Blossom on Columbus

FARTHER AFIELD
Casual
Grimaldi's
Classic NY
Peter Luger Steak House
Contemporary
Blue Ribbon Brasserie
Henry's End
Fine Dining
River Café

EAT

Eating A–Z

'21' CLUB $$$

21club.com

With a history spanning more than eight decades, this popular eatery doffs a cap to its speakeasy days. Choose from the fixed-price menus or an extensive à la carte featuring lobster, steak, salmon, seasonal produce and much more. The '21' burger is a perennial favorite.

➕ D10 ✉ 21 W 52nd Street/5th–6th avenues ☎ 212/582-7200 🕐 Mon–Fri lunch, Mon–Sat dinner 🚇 B, D, F, M 47th–50th streets–Rockefeller Center

A LA TURKA $$

alaturkarestaurant.com

A sociable neighborhood favorite for over 20 years, A La Turka's menu features grilled meats and fish, a dozen kinds of kebabs and a terrific chopped Shepherd's salad. Try the *lahmecon*, traditional Turkish pizza or one of the vegetarian specials.

➕ F7 ✉ 1417 2nd Avenue/74th Street ☎ 212/744-2424 🕐 Daily lunch and dinner 🚇 6 77th Street

THE BAILEY $$

thebaileynyc.com

Just off Wall Street, this is a big hit with the Financial District crowd. The offerings include pub favorites like fish and chips and shepherd's pie, plus a wide American menu and a selection of salads. At the busy bar you can order snacks, burgers or mac 'n' cheese while watching sports on TV.

➕ E22 ✉ 52 William Street ☎ 212/859-2200 🕐 Daily breakfast, lunch and dinner, weekend brunch 🚇 2, 3, 4, 5 Wall Street

BARNEY GREENGRASS $–$$

barneygreengrass.com

An Upper West Side tradition since 1929, this is frantic on weekends, when locals feast on huge platters of smoked fish—whitefish, sablefish, sturgeon and lox—or have the same ingredients packed into a hearty sandwich.

➕ B5 ✉ 541 Amsterdam Avenue/86th Street ☎ 212/724-4707 🕐 Tue–Fri 8.30–4, Sat–Sun 8.30–5 🚇 1 86th Street

LE BERNARDIN $$$

le-bernardin.com

Frenchman Eric Ripert is known to be the fish maestro. Exquisite, inventive dishes are served by super-attentive waiters.

➕ D10 ✉ 155 W 51st Street/7th Avenue ☎ 212/554-1515 🕐 Mon–Fri lunch, Mon–Sat dinner 🚇 B, D, F, M 47th–50th streets–Rockefeller Center

FOOD HALLS

Curated, gourmet food halls are very popular, where diners can select from different cuisines. In addition to Eataly (▷ 121–122), check out the Pennsy at Penn Station (✉ 2 Pennsylvania Plaza ☎ 917/475-1830), Grand Central Terminal (▷ 145), The Todd English Food Hall in the lower level of the Plaza Hotel (✉ 1 West 59th Street ☎ 212/986-9260) and Urbanspace Vanderbilt, outside Grand Central (✉ Corner of Vanderbilt Avenue/45th Street ☎ 646/747-0822), home to a constantly changing line-up of concept outlets.

EAT

BLOSSOM ON COLUMBUS $$

blossomnyc.com

This cozy branch of the Blossom empire boasts a selection of bio-dynamic beers and wines, and top vegan fare. The soy bacon cheese-burger has a devoted following.

 C5 ✉ 507 Columbus Avenue/84th Street ☎ 212/875-2600 ⏲ Daily lunch and dinner, weekend brunch 🚇 B, C 81st Street–Museum of Natural History

BLUE RIBBON BRASSERIE $$

blueribbonrestaurants.com

There's a Manhattan feel to this huge modern-American favorite in Brooklyn's Park Slope—not surprising, since it has a SoHo outlet also (97 Sullivan Street/Prince Street), liked by off-duty chefs. It combines the creative with comfort food.

⊞ Off map ✉ 280 5th Avenue/ 1st Street, Brooklyn ☎ 718/840-0404 ⏲ Daily dinner 🚇 R Union Street

BOAT BASIN CAFÉ $

boatbasincafe.com

It's hard to find this open-air café serving burgers, salads and sand-wiches on the banks of the Hudson but, if you do, enjoy daz-zling views from a terrace table.

⊞ A6 ✉ W 79th Street/Hudson River ☎ 212/496-5542 ⏲ Late Mar–Oct (weather permitting) daily lunch and dinner 🚇 1 79th Street

BUBBY'S $

bubbys.com

A Tribeca favorite serving Bubby's all-American BLTs, chicken clubs, meat loaf and fries, and pies, including Key lime and banoffee. Expect a wait for the popular week-end brunch.

⊞ D19 ✉ 120 Hudson Street ☎ 212/219-0666 ⏲ Daily 8am–11pm 🚇 1, 9 Franklin Street; A, C, E Canal Street

CAFÉ BOULUD $$–$$$

cafeboulud.com

This Daniel Boulud French restau-rant has classical, seasonal and ethnic influences. The prix-fixe lunches are good value and live jazz is featured on Friday nights.

⊞ E6 ✉ 20 E 76th Street/5th–Madison avenues ☎ 212/772-2600 ⏲ Daily breakfast, lunch, dinner, Sun brunch 🚇 6 77th Street

Bubby's in Tribeca is a favorite choice for weekend brunch

CARMINE'S $$

carminesnyc.com

This beloved, raucous place serves Sicilian-Italian dishes family-style—huge platters to share. It's not for picky foodies, but it's fun.

➕ B4 ✉ 2450 Broadway/90th Street ☎ 212/362-2200 🕐 Daily lunch and dinner 🚇 1, 2, 3 96th Street–Broadway

CASA LEVER $$$

casalever.com

The ocean-liner-esque design is the star at this restaurant, downstairs in the Lever House building, but it's worth a visit just for the chef's contemporary twists on northern Italian classics.

➕ E10 ✉ 390 Park Avenue/53rd Street ☎ 212/888-2700 🕐 Mon–Fri breakfast, lunch and dinner, Sat dinner 🚇 6 51st Street; E, M Lexington Avenue–53rd Street

DANIEL $$$

danielnyc.com

This formal restaurant serves modern French dishes—opt for the seven-course tasting menu to fully appreciate chef Daniel Boulud's brilliance. Dessert arrives with its own basket of warm madeleines.

➕ E8 ✉ 60 E 65th Street/Madison–Park avenues ☎ 212/288-0033 🕐 Mon–Sat dinner 🚇 6 68th Street–Hunter College

DEL POSTO $$$

delposto.com

Noted restaurateurs Joe and Lidia Bastianich created this swanky, deco-looking, big-night-out Italian restaurant, with piano player and tableside preparations.

➕ B15 ✉ 85 10th Avenue/16th Street ☎ 212/497-8090 🕐 Mon–Fri lunch and dinner, Sat–Sun dinner 🚇 A, C, E, L 14th Street

DELICATESSEN $

delicatessennyc.com

In need of some comfort food? At this funky NoLIta (North of Little Italy) restaurant you can start with cheeseburger spring rolls, followed by steak-frites.

➕ F18 ✉ 54 Prince Street/Lafayette Street ☎ 212/226-0211 🕐 Mon–Fri breakfast, lunch and dinner, Sat–Sun brunch and dinner 🚇 N, R Prince Street

DELMONICO'S $$$

delmonicosny.com

Old New York lives on at this pioneer restaurant founded in 1867, renovated but still with its old-world charm and serving excellent steaks.

➕ F22 ✉ 56 Beaver Street/William Street ☎ 212/509-1144 🕐 Lunch Mon–Fri, dinner Mon–Sat 🚇 2, 3 Wall Street; 4, 5 Bowling Green; J, Z Broad Street

ELEVEN MADISON PARK $$$

elevenmadisonpark.com

This is one of the world's finest restaurants—and one of the best in New York. Chef Daniel Humm delivers knockout tasting menus of his contemporary American cuisine

---

VEGGIE DELIGHTS

With a third of Americans now opting to eat vegetarian at least once a week, New York has become a center for creative meat-free restaurants. At the higher end are Kajitsu (▷ 146) and Blossom on Columbus (▷ 143). Veggie lovers should also seek out Peacefood Café (✉ 460 Amsterdam Avenue/82nd Street ☎ 212/362-2266) and celebrity chef Chloe Coscarelli's By Chloe (✉ 185 Bleecker Street/MacDougal Street ☎ 212/290-8000).

EAT

at stratospheric prices. Reserve well in advance.

⊞ E14 ⊠ 11 Madison Avenue/24th Street ☎ 212/889-0905 🕔 Daily dinner, Fri–Sun lunch 🚇 6, R, W 23rd Street

FORTY CARROTS $

bloomingdales.com/59th-street

Take a Midtown break at this pleasant hideaway on the 7th floor of Bloomingdales. The freshly made salads, sandwiches and soups are tasty and the frozen yogurt is the best in town.

⊞ F9 ⊠ Bloomingdales, 150 E 60th Street between Lexington/3rd avenues ☎ 212/705-3085 🕔 Daily lunch and dinner to 7.30pm 🚇 4, 5, 6 59th Street

GOTHAM BAR AND GRILL $$$

gothambarandgrill.com

This light and airy restaurant epitomizes New York grandeur, with world-class dishes such as miso-marinated black cod. The greenmarket lunch is good value.

⊞ E16 ⊠ 12 E 12th Street/5th Avenue ☎ 212/620-4020 🕔 Mon–Fri lunch and dinner, Sat–Sun dinner only 🚇 4, 5, 6, L, N, Q, R, W 14th Street–Union Square

GRIMALDI'S $

grimaldis-pizza.com

Grimaldi's dates back to 1905. Pick a basic pizza or add your own toppings for a mouthwatering masterpiece. Constant lines are testament to its reputation. Credit cards are not accepted here.

⊞ H21 ⊠ 1 Front Street (under Brooklyn Bridge) ☎ 718/858-4300 🕔 Daily lunch, dinner 🚇 2, 3 Clark Street: A, C High Street

HENRY'S END $$

henrysend.com

This neighborhood favorite in Brooklyn has high ceilings, brick

---

GRAND CENTRAL

Here are some highlights at the Dining Concourse at Grand Central Terminal:
Central Market New York makes creative, delicous sandwiches.
Café Spice for curries.
Grand Central Oyster Bar is an upscale seafood bar, with cocktails (▷ 148).
Magnolia Bakery for scrumptious pastries.
Shake Shack has world-renowned burgers plus tasty fat-top dogs and shakes.
Mendy's Kosher Delicatessen has noodle soup, knishes and pastrami-on-rye.

---

walls and an open kitchen. The menu features seasonal fish and locally sourced meat and produce, but the highlight is the Wild Game Festival (winter to spring), plus an award-winning wine list.

⊞ H22 ⊠ 44 Henry Street/Cranberry Street, Brooklyn Heights ☎ 718/834-1776 🕔 Daily dinner 🚇 2, 3 Clark Street; A, C High Street

JACKSON HOLE $

jacksonholeburgers.com

This small chain of burger places is useful when all you want is a

Casa Lever

EAT

145

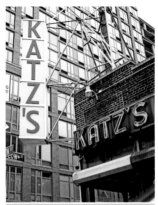
Katz's, a deli to die for

hefty sandwich in a child-friendly, no-frills environment.

🕂 F8 ✉ 232 E 64th Street/2nd Avenue ☎ 212/371-7187 🕙 Daily lunch and dinner 🚇 6 68th Street–Hunter College

JEAN-GEORGES $$$
jean-georgesrestaurant.com
One of the world's great chefs, Alsace native Jean-Georges Vongerichten is known for his refined, full-flavored Asian-accented cooking. The glass-walled minimalist rooms feel serene and special. Lunch here is a (relative) bargain.

🕂 C9 ✉ 1 Central Park West/60th Street ☎ 212/299-3900 🕙 Mon–Sat lunch and dinner, Sun dinner 🚇 1, A, B, C, D 59th Street–Columbus Circle

JOHN'S PIZZERIA $
johnspizzerianyc.com
This converted church (do look up to enjoy the beautiful stained-glass ceiling) has one of just a handful of coal brick-ovens left in the city. It's a great spot to head to for a pre- or post-theater pizza.

🕂 C11 ✉ 260 W 44th Street ☎ 212/391-7560 🕙 Daily lunch and dinner 🚇 1, 2, 3, 7, N, Q, R, S, W Times Square-42nd Street

KAJITSU $$$
kajitsunyc.com
The only vegetarian restaurant in New York to be awarded a Michelin star, Kajitsu promotes Japanese *shojin* cuisine through its multi-course tasting menus. The choices change each month, with emphasis on seasonal dishes. Reserve well in advance.

🕂 E12 ✉ 125 E 39th Street/Lexington Avenue ☎ 212/228-4873 🕙 Tue–Sun dinner 🚇 4, 5, 6, 7, S 42nd Street–Grand Central

KATZ'S DELI $
katzsdelicatessen.com
The site of the hilarious climactic scene in *When Harry Met Sally* is the last deli in a once thriving Jewish neighborhood. Opened in 1888, it upholds traditions such as plain surroundings, and serves knishes and pastrami sandwiches.

NEW YORK RESTAURANT WEEK

The best dining deal in town is no longer a mere seven-day affair. New York Restaurant Week now takes place twice a year, and lasts for up to a month each winter and summer. Participating restaurants offer three-course lunches and dinners at a set price. The cost of your drinks, tax and tip are extra. This event offers a great chance to dine at some of New York's best and hottest restaurants for a fraction of the normal price. The menus are designed to show off their classic dishes and cooking styles. Check out the dates and restaurants at nycgo.com, and book ahead—the best tables go fast!

🔲 G17 ☒ 205 E Houston Street/Ludlow Street ☎ 212/254-2246 🕐 Daily breakfast, lunch and dinner 🚇 F 2nd Avenue

THE LOEB BOATHOUSE $$

thecentralparkboathouse.com

Leave hectic Manhattan behind at this lakeside place in Central Park. The food is contemporary American but the view is the main reason for coming. The cocktail deck gets busy in summer. Reservations are advised.

🔲 D7 ☒ Central Park, nearest to E 72nd Street entrance ☎ 212/517-2233 🕐 Mon–Fri lunch and dinner, Sat–Sun brunch and dinner, lunch only Dec–Mar 🚇 6 68th Street–Hunter College

MISSION CHINESE FOOD $$$

missionchinesefood.com

This is chef Danny Bowien's NYC branch of the much-loved San Franciscan restaurant. Its current home came with a built-in pizza oven, so Bowien added the Italian staple to his menu of mostly northern Chinese cuisine. It's just a typical example of how this place bends the rules. Reservations are only accepted online.

🔲 G19 ☒ 171 East Broadway/Essex Street ☎ 917/376-5660 🕐 Daily dinner, Sat–Sun lunch 🚇 F East Broadway; J, M, Z Essex Street

MOMOFUKU SSÄM BAR $$

ssambar.momofuku.com

This Korean eatery is part of chef David Chang's Momofuku empire. The daily menu could offer anything from mason jars of kimchi to slow-roasted pork or pork chops in Asian fish sauce.

🔲 F16 ☒ 207 2nd Avenue/13th Street ☎ 212/254-3500 🕐 Daily dinner, Mon–Fri lunch, Sat–Sun brunch 🚇 L 3rd Avenue

SWEET TREATS

Treat yourself to city favorites like frozen hot chocolate or ice cream concoctions at Serendipity 3 (🔲 225 E 60th/2nd Avenue, ☎ 212/838-3351), Austrian pastries at Café Sabarsky (Neue Gallery ▷ 70) or chocolate pizza at Max Brenner (🔲 841 Broadway/13th Street, ☎ 646/467-8803).

NOBU FIFTY SEVEN $$$

noburestaurants.com

It is difficult to get a reservation at this huge Japanese restaurant, part owned by Robert de Niro, but you'll be rewarded by memorable food and polished wood and chandeliers. Choose the Kobe-style Wagyu beef, or toro tartare with caviar.

🔲 D19 ☒ 40 West 57th Street/between 5th and 6th avenues ☎ 212/757-3000 🕐 Daily lunch and dinner 🚇 57th Street

NORTH SQUARE $$

northsquareny.com

Chef Yoel Cruz's inventive cooking focuses on European and Asian-influenced dishes. The atmosphere is relaxed, and dishes such as coriander-crusted yellowfin tuna are sublime. The Sunday jazz brunch has sets at 12.30 and 2.15.

🔲 D16 ☒ 103 Waverly Place/MacDougal Street ☎ 212/254-1200 🕐 Daily breakfast and dinner, Mon–Fri lunch, Sat–Sun brunch 🚇 A, B, C, D, E, F, M West 4th Street–Washington Square

THE ODEON $$

theodeonrestaurant.com

The original hot spot of the Bright Lights, Big City age of the 1980s, this art deco-style restaurant is still going strong. Its tiled floors, dim lighting and happy bar area are some reasons why—that and

EAT

the always-reliable nouvelle American food, including all-day breakfast served through late night.
🚇 D20 ✉ 145 West Broadway/Thomas Street ☎ 212/233-0507 🕐 Daily breakfast, lunch and dinner 🚉 A, C Chambers Street

ORIENTAL GARDEN $–$$
orientalgardenny.com
There are several good reasons to visit this big, long-time Cantonese favorite in Chinatown: tasty dim sum, seafood fresh from the tanks, and very good prices.
🚇 F19 ✉ 14 Elizabeth Street/Bayard Canal ☎ 212/619-0085 🕐 Daily lunch and dinner 🚉 6, J, N, R, Q Canal Street

OYSTER BAR $$
oysterbarny.com
Some reports suggest this 1913 vaulted room in Grand Central Terminal may be resting on past glories, but for a thoroughly New York experience it's hard to beat.
🚇 E11 ✉ Grand Central Terminal, lower level ☎ 212/490-6650 🕐 Mon–Sat lunch and dinner 🚉 4, 5, 6, 7 Grand Central–42nd Street

PER SE $$$
perseny.com
Reserve *way* ahead for Thomas Keller's distinctive (and expensive) tasting menus, such as hand-cut tagliatelle with truffles, and char-coal-grilled Wagyu. Enjoy great Central Park views with your meal.
🚇 C9 ✉ Time Warner Center, 10 Columbus Circle, 4th floor/60th Street ☎ 212/823-9335 🕐 Daily dinner, Fri–Sun lunch 🚉 1, A, B, C, D 59th Street–Columbus Circle

PERSEPOLIS $$
persepolisnewyork.com
This homely, friendly restaurant serves some of the city's finest Middle Eastern cuisine. Try the delicious Persian dishes such as saffron-marinated rack of lamb, and traditional *koresht* (stews).
🚇 F7 ✉ 1407 2nd Avenue/73rd Street ☎ 212/535-1100 🕐 Daily lunch and dinner 🚉 6 68th Street–Hunter College

PETER LUGER STEAK HOUSE $$$
peterluger.com
This unpretentious steakhouse has been serving the city's best beef to hungry New Yorkers since 1887. Order hash browns and creamed spinach to accompany your steak. Reserve early. Cash or US debit cards; credit cards aren't accepted.
🚇 Off map ✉ 178 Broadway/Driggs Avenue, Brooklyn ☎ 718/387-7400 🕐 Daily lunch and dinner 🚉 J, Z Marcy Avenue

PONDICHERI $$
pondichericafe.com/location/new-york
Star Houston chef Anita Jaisinghani brings her famed Indian cooking to the Big Apple. During the day,

FOOD ON WHEELS
The lowly hot dog stand and pretzel cart have stepped up a notch. More than 3,000 gourmet food trucks now ply the streets of Manhattan, serving up a variety of tasty, healthy and inexpensive fare to busy New Yorkers on the go. Doling out everything from biryanis to Korean BBQ, organic salads to schnitzel and Belgian waffles, some have reached near-cult status. Trucks broadcast their locations to fans on Twitter, and there are websites and apps to help. One source is roaminghunger.com.

expect authentic street food and Mumbai-style sandwiches; at night, enjoy traditional *thali*.

🚩 E14 ✉ 15 West 27th Street
☎ 646/878-4375 🕐 Daily breakfast, lunch and dinner 🚇 R, W 28th Street

RIVER CAFÉ $$$

rivercafe.com

For a special occasion (jackets required, guys) and drop-dead views across the East River to Manhattan, this is a treat. Classic international food ranges from wild shrimp and rock lobster to rabbit with ricotta.

🚩 Off map ✉ 1 Water Street (under the Brooklyn Bridge) ☎ 718/522-5200
🕐 Mon–Fri breakfast and dinner, Sat lunch and dinner, Sun brunch and dinner 🚇 2, 3 Clark Street; A, C High Street

ROSA MEXICANO $$

rosamexicano.com

Popular with theater-goers, Rosa Mexicano's menu offers traditional Mexican cooking, while the David Rockwell-designed interior—including a 30ft (9m) blue-tiled wall of water—is totally contemporary.

🚩 C8 ✉ 61 Columbus Avenue/62nd Street ☎ 212/977-7700 🕐 Mon–Fri lunch, daily dinner, Sat–Sun brunch 🚇 1, A, B, C, D 59th Street–Columbus Circle

THE SPOTTED PIG $$

thespottedpig.com

You may have to wait for a table (you can't reserve) at this Michelin-starred, Anglo-style gastro pub. Order the *gnudi*, a ricotta gnocchi that chef April Bloomfield has made her own.

🚩 D16 ✉ 314 W 11th Street/Greenwich Avenue ☎ 212/620-0393 🕐 Daily lunch and dinner, Sat–Sun also brunch
🚇 1 Christopher Street

UNCLE NICK'S $$

unclenicksgreekcuisine.com

A fun atmosphere and hearty cooking are hallmarks at this West Side Greek restaurant.

🚩 B10 ✉ 747 9th Avenue/50th Street
☎ 212/245-7992 🕐 Daily lunch and dinner 🚇 C, E 50th Street

UNION SQUARE CAFÉ $$$

unionsquarecafe.com

The first of Danny Meyer's restaurant empire is one of the best, with a combination of award-winning contemporary American fare and warm ambience rarely found at this level. Note there is no tipping; hospitality is included in the price.

🚩 E15 ✉ 101 E 19th Street/Park Avenue South ☎ 212/273-4020 🕐 Daily dinner, Mon–Fri lunch, Sat–Sun brunch 🚇 4, 5, 6, L, N, Q, R 14th Street

VESELKA $

veselka.com

Dine here at any time of day or night on traditional Ukrainian and soul food. The menu ranges from handmade *pierogi* (dumplings) to goulash and *blintzes*.

🚩 F16 ✉ 144 2nd Avenue/E 9th Street
☎ 212/228-9682 🕐 Daily 24 hours 🚇 6 Astor Place; F 2nd Avenue; R, W 8th Street

EAT

Sleep

With options ranging from the luxurious to simple budget hotels, New York has accommodations to suit everyone. In this section establishments are listed alphabetically.

SLEEP

Introduction

New York has hundreds of hotels, but like most major cities, prices are high and spaces are tight. Here are some tips to help you choose wisely.

What to Expect

In a city where space is at a premium, your room may be smaller than you had hoped but there is no shortage of amenities. Most budget hotels offer private baths, TV and air conditioning, hair dryers and coffee makers. Many have a fitness facility. In luxury hotels, you can expect daily newspapers, robes, spas, room service and a concierge to make reservations and help you navigate the city.

Do the Research

Finding comfortable affordable lodgings is a challenge. Make use of discounted reservation sites like trivago.com or kayak.com, which compare prices from several sites. Rates are usually lower on weekends when business travelers go home. Hotel websites often offer discounts if you reserve for three days or more and may have seasonal specials and weekend packages. When calculating costs, remember that quoted rates usually do not include taxes, which will add about 15 percent to your bill.

Some Saving Tips

Airbnb.com, bedandbreakfast.com and similar services are a growing option. Some also offer apartments that are good deals for families. Look for hotels with complimentary breakfast and evening meal. And free WiFi is a bonus.

HOME AWAY FROM HOME

One way to stretch your travel budget is to consider a home stay or apartment swap. HomeExchange.com (for a fee) will help you swap homes with New Yorkers. VRBO.com is another reputable source for short-term apartment rentals.

From top: The Plunge Bar and Lounge at Hotel Gansevoort; guest room in the Shoreham; Crosby Street Hotel; The New York Edition lobby

Directory

LOWER MANHATTAN
Mid-Range
Off Soho Suites
Luxury
Crosby Street Hotel
Ritz-Carlton Battery Park

DOWNTOWN AND CHELSEA
Budget
Carlton Arms
Hotel 17
Mid-Range
Maritime Hotel
Washington Square
Luxury
Hotel Gansevoort
The Inn at Irving Place

MIDTOWN
Budget
Ameritania Hotel
Hotel Wolcott
Pod 51
Mid-Range
Casablanca

citizenM
Hotel Eventi
The Hudson
Iberostar 70 Park Avenue
Library Hotel
Millennium Broadway
The New York Edition
The Shoreham
The Time
Luxury
Four Seasons
Mandarin Oriental
The Plaza
St. Regis

UPPER WEST SIDE
Budget
Hotel Belleclaire
Mid-Range
Excelsior
Hotel Beacon

FARTHER AFIELD
Luxury
1 Hotel Brooklyn Bridge

Sleeping A–Z

PRICES
Prices are approximate and based on a double room for one night.

$$$	over $450
$$	$251–$450
$	$150–$250

1 HOTEL BROOKLYN BRIDGE $$$
1hotels.com
This new stylish boutique hotel in DUMBO (Down Under the Manhattan Bridge Overpass) has expansive waterfront views of the East River and Manhattan skyline. It was designed by local artists using reclaimed wood, and there's a rooftop pool also.
🚇 Off map ✉ 60 Furman Street
☎ 877/803-1111 🚉 Brooklyn Bridge

AMERITANIA HOTEL $
ameritanianyc.com
If you want to be in the heart of the theater district then this Times Square hotel in a Beaux Arts building, provides mid-class accommodations with spacious common areas and lounge bar.
🚇 C10 ✉ 230 W 54th Street/Broadway
☎ 212/247-5000 🚉 N, Q, R, W 57th Street–7th Avenue

CARLTON ARMS $

carltonarms.com

Decorated with crazy murals in the lobby and some rooms, this is one of New York's wackiest hotels, close to Madison Square. Amenities are minimal but there is a communal, boho atmosphere that makes visitors feel at home. As it says on the business card, "this ain't no Holiday Inn."

➕ F14 ✉ 160 E 25th Street/Lexington–3rd avenues ☎ 212/679-0680
🚇 6 23rd Street

CASABLANCA $$

casablancahotel.com

Moroccan prints and tiles make this small, family-owned boutique hotel an oasis of color and style. Rooms range from cozy classics to premium kings and mini-suites, all with luxurious bath amenities and complimentary WiFi. Deluxe continental breakfast and passes to New York Sports Club are included.

➕ D11 ✉ 147 W 43rd Street/7th Avenue ☎ 212/869-1212 🚇 1, 2, 3, 7, N, Q, R, S, W Times Square–42nd Street

CITIZENM $–$$

citizenm.com

Mood pads—high-tech controls in rooms that manage the lights, TV and window blinds—are among many reasons visitors come to this happening Dutch import. A rooftop bar just for guests, a state-of-the-art 20th-floor gym with views and a big jazzy living-room lobby with a 24-hour bar/café add to the attractions. The rooms are as tight as a ship's cabin but with king-size beds and picture windows. WiFi and movies are free; join the citizenM Club for room discounts.

➕ D10 ✉ 218 W 50th Street ☎ 212/461-3638 🚇 1, C, E 50th Street

CROSBY STREET HOTEL $$$

crosbystreethotel.com

Located in the heart of vibrant SoHo, the 86 rooms and suites over 11 floors have full-length warehouse-style windows. The interior design by Kit Kemp is fresh and contemporary, and the hotel has a gym, cinema and a sculpture garden, as well as a selection of one- and two-bedroom suites.

The bar in Crosby Street Hotel, a fashionable choice in SoHo

The Ty Warner Penthouse in the Four Seasons

🕂 E18 ✉ 79 Crosby Street, between Prince and Spring streets ☎ 212/226-6400 🚇 4, 6 Spring Street–Lafayette Street

EXCELSIOR $$

excelsiorhotelny.com

The location is fabulous—steps from Central Park and the American Museum of Natural History. The building is old-fashioned, with wood paneling, faux-oils and gilt frames. Rooms, though not beautiful, are fine, especially the standard rooms that overlook the park.

🕂 C6 ✉ 45 W 81st Street/Columbus ☎ 212/362-9200 🚇 B, C 81st Street–Museum of Natural History

FOUR SEASONS $$$

fourseasons.com/newyork

The grandiose I.M. Pei building makes a big first impression—all towering lobbies, marble and mezzanine lounges, plus Ty Bar. The rooms don't disappoint. They're big, with tons of closets, tubs that fill in no time and, in some, great views. Many consider this Manhattan's top hotel.

🕂 E9 ✉ 57 E 57th Street, Park–Madison avenues ☎ 212/758-5700 🍴 The Garden, TY Bar 🚇 N, R 5th Avenue

HOTEL 17 $

hotel17ny.com

The kitschy decor almost seems deliberate—its stripy wallpaper and floral bedspreads seem to hit a

chord with fashionable types. That could also be on account of its brownstone Gramercy Park location and low rates, plus free WiFi and coffee machines. All rooms have shared bathrooms.

🕂 F15 ✉ 225 E 17th Street/2nd–3rd avenues ☎ 212/475-2845 🚇 L 3rd Avenue

HOTEL BEACON $$

beaconhotel.com

In the middle of Broadway, on the Upper West Side, the Beacon feels more like an apartment building than a hotel. All rooms here have kitchenettes, plus free WiFi.

🕂 B7 ✉ 2130 Broadway/75th Street ☎ 212/787-1100 🚇 1, 2, 3 72nd Street

HOTEL BELLECLAIRE $$

hotelbelleclaire.com

Mark Twain lived here, as did Maxim Gorky, and Babe Ruth was a notable guest. This early 20th-century building offers fabulously decorated guest rooms that maintain some of their historic charm, while being thoroughly modern.

🕂 B6 ✉ 250 W 77th Street/Broadway ☎ 212/362-7700 🚇 1 79th Street

HOTEL EVENTI $$

hoteleventi.com

This stylish Chelsea hotel has a hospitable sitting room-lobby where morning coffee and evening wine are offered. Rooms have contemporary decor, floor-to-ceiling windows for city views and rainfall

SLEEP

B&BS

Those who'd like to experience the city more like a local may opt to stay in a B&B, of which there are plenty in all five boroughs. Often located in historic brownstones in charming neighborhoods, many offer great prices and the quality of the rooms can be as good if not better than some hotels. (Be aware, however, that some B&Bs don't actually include the second B, breakfast.) Visit bedandbreakfast.com or airbnb.com for listings.

Rooftop pool at Hotel Gansevoort

HOTEL WOLCOTT $$
wolcott.com
Within walking distance of the Empire State Building, this hotel has comfortable rooms with private bath, plus free breakfast and fitness center.
➕ D13 ✉ 4 W 31st Street, between 5th Avenue and Broadway ☎ 212/268-2900 🚇 B, D, F, M, N, Q, R, W 34th Street–Herald Square

THE HUDSON $$
hudsonhotel.com
All subdued lighting and minimalist chic, the Hudson is close to Central Park. It comes alive at night with a popular cocktail bar and lounge, a rooftop terrace, and there is a basement gym. Request a room (tiny, even by NY standards) overlooking the atrium, as these tend to be much quieter.
➕ B9 ✉ 358 W 58th Street/Columbus Avenue ☎ 212/554-6000 🚇 1, A, B, C, D 59th Street–Columbus Circle

showers in the marble bathrooms. The Vine bar, with a 24-hour menu and L'Amico, an Italian restaurant, are on the premises.
➕ D13 ✉ 851 6th Avenue/29th Street ☎ 212/564-4567 🚇 1 28th Street; F 34th Street

HOTEL GANSEVOORT $$$
hotelgansevoort.com
A stylish hotel that's packed with facilities; these include a rooftop pool, a spa, the Chester restaurant and bar, and the Plunge rooftop bar and lounge. The guest rooms are furnished in stone and sand colors and equipped with high-tech gadgets. There's a sister hotel on Park Avenue.
➕ C16 ✉ 18 9th Avenue/13th Street ☎ 212/206-6700 🚇 A, C, E 14th Street; L 8th Avenue

IBEROSTAR 70 PARK AVENUE $$
70parkave.com
This large place in Midtown's Murray Hill has a quietly contemporary decor, luxurious extras such as touch-screen room service, a pillow menu, good sound systems and a 24-hour fitness center.
➕ E12 ✉ 70 Park Avenue/38th Street ☎ 212/973-2400 🍴 Silverleaf Tavern 🚇 4, 5, 6, 7, S Grand Central–42nd Street

LOCATION, LOCATION, LOCATION
Thinking about how you plan to spend your time in New York can help you find the best neighborhood in which to stay. Seeing theater every night? A hotel within walking distance of Times Square will be a real plus. Love people-watching? The Upper West Side is great for strolling and hotels are within easy reach of Central Park. Shopping? Check out a Lower Manhattan hotel near SoHo's many stores.

SLEEP

THE INN AT IRVING PLACE $$$

innatirving.com

This discreet hotel (there's no name outside) is set in two 1830s town houses near Gramercy Park, with elegant decor, period furniture and open fireplaces. The intimate size and period styling make you feel like you've stepped into a Merchant Ivory film.

➕ E15 ✉ 56 Irving Place/17th Street ☎ 212/533-4600 🚇 4, 5, 6, L, N, Q, R, W Union Square

LIBRARY HOTEL $$

libraryhotel.com

Each of the 10 floors of the hotel is dedicated to a subject category from the Dewey Decimal System, and each room has a collection of related art and books. The interior is modern and minimalist. The Reading Room is the venue of complimentary breakfast and evening wine-and-cheese receptions, and the poetry garden is a charming and relaxing oasis.

➕ E11 ✉ 299 Madison Avenue/41st Street ☎ 212/983-4500 🚇 4, 5, 6, 7, S Grand Central–42nd Street

MANDARIN ORIENTAL $$$

mandarinoriental.com/newyork

The Mandarin Oriental, built upward from the 35th floor, offers stunning city panoramas. The best of the luxurious rooms and suites have floor-to-ceiling views looking across Central Park or over the Hudson. The hotel also has a luxury spa and wellness center.

➕ C9 ✉ 80 Columbus Circle/60th Street ☎ 212/805-8800 🍴 Asiate 🚇 1, A, B, C, D 59th Street–Columbus Circle

MARITIME HOTEL $$

themaritimehotel.com

Right in the thick of the Meatpacking District, this is where quirky meets effortless style. Porthole windows facing the Hudson and navy-blue soft furnishings add to the ship-like feel of the decor. Facilities include a fitness center, a happening bar scene and an Asian-fusion restaurant. Guests can also make use of the complimentary bicycles for sightseeing.

➕ C15 ✉ 363 W 16th Street/9th Avenue ☎ 212/242-4300 🍴 Tao Downtown 🚇 A, C, E 14th Street

View over the Hudson from the Mandarin Oriental

MILLENNIUM BROADWAY $$

millenniumhotels.com

Close to many Broadway shows, plus Times Square, the Millennium is a good choice for theater-lovers. The high-ceilinged lobby leads to a 52-story building, with 750 guest rooms, and suites that have floor-to-ceiling windows for great views.

➕ D11 ✉ 145 W 44th Street/Broadway ☎ 212/768-4400 🚇 1, 2, 3 ,7, N, Q, R, S, W Times Square–42nd Street

THE NEW YORK EDITION $$$

editionhotels.com

This luxury hotel is housed in a 1909, 41-story clocktower with jaw-dropping views. Rooms are in elegant wood tones. It also has a flagship restaurant from Michelin-starred chef Jason Atherton.

➕ E14 ✉ 5 Madison Avenue/E 24th Street ☎ 212/413-4200 🚇 N, R 23rd Street

OFF SOHO SUITES $$

offsoho.com

Since opening 20 years ago, this hotel's very off-SoHo location (on the Lower East Side bordering Nolita) has become all the rage.

The suites are mini-studio apartments with modern no-fuss decor, full kitchen facilities, private phones and satellite TV. The Economy suites share a kitchen and bathroom.

➕ F18 ✉ 11 Rivington Street/Bowery ☎ 212/979-9815 🚇 F 2nd Avenue; J, Z Bowery

THE PLAZA $$$

theplazany.com

With suites and rooms overlooking Fifth Avenue or Central Park, The Plaza is one of the city's more expensive hotels.

➕ D9 ✉ 5th Avenue at Central Park South ☎ 212/759-3000 🚇 N, R, W 5th Avenue--59th Street

POD 51 $

thepodhotel.com

Rooms are small but the rates are competitive. Some rooms share baths, some have bunk beds popular with families. Check the website for other locations.

➕ F10 ✉ 230 E 51st Street/2nd–3rd avenues ☎ 844/763-7666 🚇 6 51st Street/M 53rd Street

The St. Regis in Midtown

RITZ-CARLTON BATTERY PARK $$$

ritzcarlton.com

This glass-sided tower has views of New York Harbor and the Statue of Liberty. Decor is pale and contemporary, and the service and facilities are exemplary.

✚ D23 ✉ 2 West Street/Battery Place ☎ 212/344-0800 🚇 1 South Ferry

ST. REGIS $$$

stregisnewyork.com

Offering opulent Louis XV style in the middle of Midtown, this hotel has extremely plush rooms and suites and gives discreet service.

✚ E9–E10 ✉ 2 E 55th Street/5th Avenue ☎ 212/753-4500 🚇 E, M 5th Avenue–53rd Street

THE SHOREHAM $$

shorehamhotel.com

The Shoreham has small but tasteful rooms and suites, with the choice rooms at the back. Extras such as Aveda products, free coffee and a hotel-curated art gallery, plus high-end tech in the better rooms, add good value.

✚ D10 ✉ 33 W 55th Street/5th–6th avenues ☎ 855/212-6773 🚇 B, D, E 57th Street

THE TIME $$$

thetimeny.com

In the heart of the theater district, the hotel has newly designed rooms by David Rockwell, done in light woods with a clean modern look. Guests enjoy complimentary breakfast, daytime tea and coffee, evening wine and cheese.

✚ C11 ✉ 224 W 49th Street/between Broadway and 8th Avenue ☎ 212/246-5252 🚇 1, 2, 3, 7, N, Q, R, S, W Times Square–42nd Street

WASHINGTON SQUARE $$

washingtonsquarehotel.com

The only hotel in the heart of Greenwich Village is a firm favorite of musicians and artists. The small but smart rooms have retro furniture, while the beautiful lobby has a bright 1930s Parisian air and friendly staff. Extras include complimentary breakfast, WiFi and gym.

✚ E16 ✉ 103 Waverley Place/MacDougal Street ☎ 212/777-9515 🚇 A, B, C, D, E, F, M 4th Street–Washington Square

The Shoreham's bar

SLEEP

106 TRACKS 105

Need to Know

This section takes you through all the practical aspects of your trip to make it run more smoothly and to give you confidence before you go and while you are there.

NEED TO KNOW

Planning Ahead

WHEN TO GO

New York is at its best on crisp sunny days. Summer can be humid, but hot spells generally do not last more than a few days, and the city is bursting with activity. Fall is generally the best time to visit. Winter may bring the occasional snowstorm, but it is the least crowded and most economical season to visit.

TIME

New York is on Eastern Standard Time, three hours ahead of Los Angeles and five hours behind the UK.

TEMPERATURE

JAN	FEB	MAR	APR	MAY	JUN	JUL	AUG	SEP	OCT	NOV	DEC
39°F	41°F	46°F	61°F	70°F	81°F	84°F	82°F	77°F	66°F	54°F	39°F
4°C	5°C	8°C	16°C	21°C	27°C	29°C	28°C	25°C	19°C	12°C	4°C

Spring (March to May) is unpredictable—even in April snow showers can alternate with shirtsleeves weather—but the worst of winter is over by mid-March.

Summer (June to August) sees many pleasant days in the 80s, but be prepared for spells of heat and humidity, especially in August.

Fall (September to November) sees warm temperatures persisting into October.

Winter (December to February) varies. Some years can bring cold and snow, others can be quite mild.

WHAT'S ON

January/February *Chinese New Year* (Chinatown).

February *Westminster Kennel Club Dog Show* (☎ 212/213-3165).

March 17 *St. Patrick's Day Parade* (5th Avenue, 44th–86th streets).

March/April *Easter Parade* (5th Avenue, 44th–57th streets).

April–October *Baseball season.*

May *9th Avenue International Food Festival* (9th Avenue, 37th–57th streets ☎ 212/581-7217).

June *Metropolitan Opera park concerts* (☎ 212/362-6000).

Lesbian and Gay Pride Parade (52nd Street and 5th Avenue to Christopher and Greenwich streets).

June–September *Shakespeare in the Park* (Delacorte Theater ☎ 212/539-8750).

NY Philharmonic park concerts.

July 4 *Independence Day.*

July–August *Harlem Week* (☎ 212/862-8745).

Lincoln Center Out-of-Doors Festival (☎ 212/875-5000).

August–September *US Open Tennis Championships* (☎ 718/760-6200).

September *Feast of San Gennaro* (Little Italy).

September–October *New York Film Festival* (Lincoln Center ☎ 212/875-5601).

October *Columbus Day Parade* (5th Avenue, 44th–79th streets).

November *NYC Marathon* (Staten Island to Central Park, nycmarathon.org).

Macy's Thanksgiving Day Parade (✉ Central Park West, 77th Street ☎ 212/494-4495).

December *Tree Lighting Ceremony* (✉ Rockefeller Center ☎ 212/332-6868).

New Year's Eve celebrations (✉ Times Square).

NEW YORK ONLINE

nycgo.com
The official tourism website, linked to the NYC Information Center in Midtown, includes a calendar of events, accommodations information, news updates and lots more. The helpful trip-planning section includes themed itineraries.

broadway.org
The Broadway League's official site, with up-to-date information on shows, theaters and the theater district in several languages.

newyorkcityanswers.com
Want to know what books to read before you get to the city? Which are the best tours? Tips and tricks from native New Yorkers? This aptly named site tells all.

nyc.gov
As the official homepage of the City of New York, the site offers links to the Office of the Mayor as well as information about community services, legal policies, city agencies, news and weather and visitor information.

nyc-arts.org
With a comprehensive calendar ranging from lectures about architecture to whether the circus is in town, NYC-ARTS lives up to its catchphrase as "the complete guide."

nymag.com
One of the most comprehensive websites covering what's on in the city, including good restaurant and theater reviews.

nytimes.com
Here you'll get an inside look at New York from one of the world's most respected newspapers. The site has links to sections covering everything from world affairs to sports.

timessquarenyc.org
All about Times Square and the surrounding area, Broadway and its theaters in particular, with booking information.

TRAVEL SITES

fodors.com
A complete travel-planning site. You can research prices and weather, book air tickets, cars and rooms, pose questions to fellow travelers and find links to other sites.

iloveny.com
Official NY State site. Information about touring the city and beyond.

mta.info
The Metropolitan Transportation Authority updates you on service changes and disruptions, and answers questions about buses and the subway.

INTERNET ACCESS

WiFi is becoming more ubiquitous in New York all the time (in parks, cafés, libraries and most hotels), but it's still remarkable how many places aren't equipped—or charge a fee. Check nycgo.com/articles/wifi-in-nyc for up-to-date information. The MTA is bringing WiFi to many subway stations; look for the logo as you enter the station. The subways themselves aren't equipped...at least not yet.

Getting There

ARRIVING BY LAND

● Greyhound buses from across the US and Canada and commuter buses from New Jersey arrive at the Port Authority Terminal (✉ 625 8th Avenue ☎ 212/564-8484, greyhound.com).

● Commuter trains use Grand Central Terminal (✉ E 42nd Street/Park Avenue ☎ 212/532-4900, grandcentralterminal.com).

● Long-distance trains and New Jersey commuter trains arrive at Pennsylvania Station (✉ 31st Street/ 8th Avenue).

CUSTOMS

● Non-US citizens may import duty-free: 1 liter of alcohol (this is the total allowance for wine and/or spirits), 200 cigarettes or 50 cigars and $100 of gifts. (No one under 21 can import alcohol.)

● Among restricted items for import are meat, fruit, plants, seeds and certain prescription medicines without a prescription or written statement from your doctor.

SECURITY

● Always allow plenty of time for clearing security when arriving in or departing from the US.

AIRPORTS

New York has three airports—John F. Kennedy (JFK) (✉ Queens, 15 miles/24km east of Manhattan ☎ 718/244-4444), Newark (✉ New Jersey, 16 miles/26km west ☎ 973/961-6000) and LaGuardia (✉ Queens, 8 miles/13km east ☎ 718/533-3400). Most international flights arrive at JFK. For details, visit panynj.gov.

LaGuardia Airport 8 miles (13km) to city center. Bus/minibus 40–60 minutes, $16

Manhattan

24km (15 miles) • 16km (10 miles) • 8km (5 miles)

Newark Liberty International Airport 16 miles (26km) to city center. Bus/minibus 40–60 minutes, $17

JFK International Airport 15 miles (24km) to city center. Bus/minibus 1 hour, $19

ENTRY REQUIREMENTS

Visitors to New York from outside the US must have a full passport valid for the length of their stay and a return ticket. Under the Visa Waiver Program (VWP), visitors from most European countries, Australia, New Zealand, Japan and others do not need a visa to enter the US for stays of up to 90 days. For a full, current list of these countries, and any persons who may be excluded, check the US State Department website travel.state.gov, under "US Visa."

All VWP visitors must have machine-readable passports, and all passports issued or renewed after October 26, 2006 must be e-passports containing additional biometric information. Children and infants must each have their own passport; they cannot be included on a parent's passport.

All visitors are required to obtain an electronic authorization to travel at least 72 hours prior to departure. Registration must be done under the Electronic System for Travel Authorization (ESTA™), part of the US Department of Homeland Security. (Visitors who possess a current, valid visa do not need to fill out the ESTA™ application.) Visitors who do not obtain ESTA™ clearance at least

72 hours in advance can be denied boarding or entry to the US. For more information and to fill out the application (in several languages), go to the ESTA™ website: esta.cbp.dhs.gov/esta/. Further information is available on: cbp.gov/travel/international-visitors/esta.

There is a $14 fee payable for the ESTA™ authorization for all visitors in the VWP (▷ panel, right). Payment must be made by credit or debit card, or PayPal, when filling out the application online. The authorization is valid for two years from the date of arrival in the US.

FROM JFK
The journey to Manhattan takes around an hour. NYC Airporter express bus (tel 718/777-5111) runs every 20–30 minutes, 5am–11.30pm ($19). The SuperShuttle (▷ panel, right) runs to Manhattan 24 hours a day ($25). To reserve a place, use the courtesy telephone next to the Ground Transportation Desk. Taxis cost $52 plus tolls and tip; use the official taxi stand. The AirTrain to Jamaica (E, J, Z subway and Long Island Railroad) or Howard Beach (A subway) costs $7.75 and takes 12 minutes, plus 35–75 minutes to Midtown. It runs every 5–10 minutes, 24 hours a day.

FROM NEWARK
It takes approximately 40 to 60 minutes to get to Manhattan. AirTrain (tel 888/397-4636) goes direct from all terminals 24 hours a day to Newark airport station, from which NJ Transit operates to Penn Station in Manhattan. SuperShuttle (▷ panel, right) runs a minibus to Midtown 24 hours a day ($17). A taxi costs $50–$80, plus tolls and a $20 surcharge from Manhattan.

FROM LAGUARDIA
The journey from LaGuardia Airport to Manhattan takes between 40 and 60 minutes. SuperShuttle (▷ panel, right) runs a shared minibus 24 hours (cost $20). Services to Manhattan are also provided by NYC Airporter (cost $16; ▷ above). Taxis cost $25–$37 to Manhattan, plus tolls and tip.

ESTA™ ADVISORY
Since the introduction of the ESTA™ requirement and fee, a number of third-party websites have sprung up offering to process the application. These often charge several times the actual ESTA™ fee and are not authorized by the US government. Travelers should be sure to use only the official ESTA™ website, and pay only the $14 fee. A relative or travel agent may submit an ESTA™ application on behalf of a traveler who is unable to do it themselves.

SUPERSHUTTLE
The SuperShuttle is a shared van service that offers efficient and inexpensive door-to-door service from New York's major airports to hotels, businesses and private residences throughout the city. You may have a slightly longer journey time if your stop is at the end of the driver's route, but the set fare can be less than half the cost of a taxi. It is not essential to book in advance; you can simply turn up at the Ground Transportation Desk and wait for the next available shuttle. However, booking in advance online or by app saves time at the airport. You can also book by phone, and ask about any special promotional discounts that may apply:
☎ 1-800/258-3826, supershuttle.com.

Getting Around

LOST PROPERTY

● You are unlikely to recover items, but try the following (or call 311, city helpline):

Subway and bus
☎ 212/712-4500

Taxi
☎ 311

JFK
☎ 718/244-4225

LaGuardia
☎ 718/662-5043

Newark
☎ 908/787-0667

Report a loss quickly if claiming on your insurance.

SUBWAY TIPS

● If your Metrocard doesn't work, don't go to a different turnstile or you'll lose a fare. As the display says, you should "swipe again."

● Check the circular signs on the outside of the cars to make sure you're boarding the correct train. Often two lines share a platform.

● Look at the boards above your head to check whether you're on the up- or down-town side and/or on the local or express track.

TAXIS

NYC–Licenced Taxis
nyc.gov/taxi

Carmel Car and Limousine
☎ 212/666-6666

Dial 7 Car and Limousine
☎ 212/777-7777

BUSES

● Bus stops are near corners, marked by a sign and a yellow painted curb. Any ride costs the same as the subway–use a Metrocard or correct change ($2.75 in exact cash, or $3 SingleRide ticket sold at vending machines only).

● Bus maps are available from token booth clerks in subway stations.

● Buses are safe and clean but can be very slow during rush hour. The fastest are Select Buses. For these limited-stop buses, swipe your Metrocard at the fare kiosk before boarding.

● If you pay by Metrocard you may transfer free from bus to subway or bus to bus within two hours of the time you paid the fare.

SUBWAY

● New York subway lines often close or are diverted for maintenance on weekends, especially in Lower Manhattan and Brooklyn. Check the latest information (24 hours) before you travel (tel 511 or 718/330-1234, mta. info). New York's subway has 27 routes and 472 stations, many open 24 hours (those with a green globe outside are always staffed).

● Visit tripplanner.mta.info for accurate point-to-point subway directions.

● To ride the subway you need a Metrocard, which you can refill. Swipe the card to enter the turnstile. Refillable Metrocards are more economical than buying SingleRide tickets, and you can share the card with a companion. You can top up the card at ticket machines inside the stations. The best deals are weekly or monthly Metrocards, but these can't be shared.

● Many stations have separate entrances for up- and downtown services, often on opposite corners of the street. Check the subway map and listen to the platform announcements to determine if a train is local or express and will stop at your station.

● Children under 44in (112cm) tall ride free.

● Subways run all night, with many lines (such as the 1, 2, 3, 4, 5, 6) still crowded until well after midnight. Late-night riders should avoid less popular routes and always stay in the "off hour waiting area" until the train arrives.

TAXIS

● The ubiquitous yellow cab is a New York trademark and, except possibly on very wet or busy evenings, very easy to hail. Hotel concierges can arrange one. However, they are now outnumbered by vehicles from Uber and Lyft, which can be ordered from phone apps if you have an account.

● Another option is Via, a ride-sharing service with very economical rates for those who open accounts. The competition has caused taxis to form their own cars-on-demand site for smart phones called Curb.

● All taxis now accept credit cards: tips can be included.

DRIVING

● Driving in New York is not recommended.

● The address of the nearest major car-rental outlet can be found by calling the following toll-free numbers:

Avis, tel 800/230-4898
Budget, tel 800/218-7992
Hertz, tel 800/654-3131
National, tel 800/121-8303.

● If driving in New York is unavoidable, make sure you understand the restrictions because penalties for infringements are stringent.

● In many streets parking alternates daily from one side to the other, and it is illegal to park within 10ft (3m) either side of a fire hydrant. A car illegally parked will be towed away and the driver heavily fined. Parking is expensive.

● Within the city limits the speed limit is 25mph (40kph); right turns at a red light are prohibited.

● Passing a stopped school bus is illegal and stiff fines can be imposed.

WALKING

New York is a great city for walking. If the weather is dry (if it isn't, umbrella vendors soon materialize), it's far nicer (and often faster) to hike a 10- or 20-block distance than to take the subway, or sit in a cab or bus stalled in traffic. To work it out, figure one minute per short block (north–south) and four per long block (east–west, on cross streets).

OUTER BOROUGHS

Subway lines that appear to be identical in Manhattan often diverge in other boroughs, so make certain you know which line goes to your stop. Every major subway line goes through Manhattan except the G, which serves Queens and Brooklyn exclusively.

VISITORS WITH DISABILITIES

City law requires that all facilities constructed after 1987 provide complete access to people with disabilities. Many owners of older buildings have willingly added disability-access features as well. An important resource is the Mayor's Office for People with Disabilities (✉ 100 Gold Street, 2nd floor, 10038 ☎ 311 (ask for the office), nyc.gov/mopd. The website has information on transportation, theater, movies, concerts, parks and sport. An older comprehensive guide can be downloaded at: home2.nyc.gov/html/mopd/down loads/pdf/accessibility_guide.pdf. The city's online tourist guide, nycgo.com, has information about accessibility. Broadway guidelines are available at theatreaccess.nyc ☎ 212/912-9770). For Lincoln Center information lct.org/visit/accessibility.

Essential Facts

VISITOR INFORMATION

The city runs visitor information centers and kiosks around town. The most comprehensive is at Macy's ⊠ Herald Square ☎ 212/695-4400, nycgo.com ⏰ Mon–Sat 10–10, Sun 10–9. Other centers: ⊠ Times Square Plaza ⏰ Daily 8–7, and ⊠ City Hall ⏰ Daily 9–6. Touch screens allow visitors to research attractions and the center offers discount coupons, including to Macy's.

EMERGENCY NUMBERS

- Police, Fire Department, Ambulance ☎ 911
- Crime Victims Hotline ☎ 212/577-7777
- Sex Crimes Report Line ☎ 212/227-3000

URGENT CARE CLINICS

Doctor-manned urgent care facilities, open 24 hours daily without appointment, have opened in almost every city neighborhood. Ask at your hotel or check citymd.com for the location of one of the major groups.

ELECTRICITY

- The supply is 120 volts, 60 hz AC current.
- US appliances use flat two-prong plugs. European appliances require an adapter and a voltage transformer.

ETIQUETTE

- Tipping: waitstaff get 15–20 percent (roughly double the 8.875 percent sales tax); so do cab drivers. Bartenders get about the same (though less than $1 is stingy). Bellhops ($1 per bag), room service waiters (10 percent) and hairdressers (15–20 percent) should also be tipped.
- There are stringent smoking laws in New York. Smoking is banned on public transportation, in cabs, in all places of work, including restaurants and bars, and, since 2011, in all city parks, on beaches and in Times Square.

MAIL AND TELEPHONES

- There are many post offices dotted through the city, especially in Manhattan. Visit usps.com to find neighborhood branches.
- Stamps are also available from hotel concierges, online at usps.com, at some delis and from vending machines in stores.
- All New York numbers require the area code (212, 718, 646, 347 or 917) when dialing. For all calls, add 1 before the code. 011 is the international dialing code.
- Hotels often levy surcharges for making calls.
- Foreign visitors: watch out for mobile roaming charges that can result in a large bill on your return home; it's best to ask your mobile provider for information on data plans that can be used in the United States.
- To call the US from the UK, dial 001. To call the UK from the US, dial 011 44, then drop the first zero from the area code.

MEDICAL TREATMENT

- It is essential to have adequate insurance.
- In the event of an emergency, the 911 operator will send an ambulance.
- Doctors on Call operate 24 hours (tel 718/238-2100).

• Near Midtown, 24-hour emergency rooms: Mt. Sinai Roosevelt Hospital,10th Avenue and 59th Street, tel 212/523-4000.

• For any dental emergency any time of day or night, contact Dental Emergency Service, tel 347/282-2611.

MONEY MATTERS

• Credit cards are widely accepted. Visa, MasterCard, American Express, Diner's Card and Discover are the ones that are most commonly used.

• US dollar traveler's checks are hard to use outside hotels and currency exchange offices. It is difficult to exchange foreign currency traveler's checks, even at banks, and fees are high.

NEWSPAPERS AND MAGAZINES

• The local papers are the *New York Times* (with a Sunday edition), the *Daily News* (also with Sunday supplements) and the *New York Post*. The free alternative paper the *Village Voice* includes extensive listings. The *Wall Street Journal*, once solely a financial daily, now covers the arts scene in New York on a par with the *New York Times*.

• Pick up the *New Yorker* and *New York* magazine on newsstands; the glossier monthly magazines *In New York* and *Where* can be found in hotels, and both showcase events.

• Monday to Friday, the free dailies *amNewYork* and *Metro New York* are handed out at virtually every Manhattan subway station, and have both news and event listings.

OPENING HOURS

• Banks: Mon–Fri 9–3 or 3.30; some are open longer, and on Saturday.

• Stores: Mon–Sat 10–6; many are open far later, and on Sunday 12–6; those in the Village, Nolita and SoHo open and close later.

• Museums: hours vary, but Monday is the most common closing day.

• Post offices: Mon–Fri 8 or 9–6. Some open Sat 9–4.

• Opening times are for general guidance only.

MONEY

The unit of currency is the dollar (= 100 cents). Bills (notes) come in denominations of $1, $2, $5, $10, $20, $50 and $100; coins come in 25¢ (a quarter), 10¢ (a dime), 5¢ (a nickel) and 1¢ (a penny). Note: American coins are not marked with numerals (for example the 25 cent piece says "quarter dollar" only).

TRAVEL INSURANCE

A minimum of $1 million medical cover is advised. Choose a policy that covers baggage and document loss, and cancellation.

PUBLIC HOLIDAYS

• New Year's Day: January 1
• Martin Luther King, Jr. Day: third Monday of January
• Presidents' Day: third Monday of February
• Memorial Day: last Monday in May
• Independence Day: July 4
• Labor Day: first Monday in September
• Columbus Day: second Monday in October
• Veterans' Day: November 11
• Thanksgiving Day: fourth Thursday of November
• Christmas Day: December 25

CONSULATES

Australia
✉ 150 E 42nd Street
☎ 212/351-6500
Canada
✉ 1251 6th Avenue
☎ 212/596-1628
Denmark
✉ 885 2nd Avenue,
18th Floor
☎ 212/223-4545
France
✉ 934 5th Avenue
☎ 212/606-3600
Germany
✉ 871 UN Plaza
☎ 212/610-9700
Ireland
✉ 345 Park Avenue
☎ 212/319-2555
Italy
✉ 690 Park Avenue
☎ 212/737-9100
Norway
✉ 825 3rd Avenue
☎ 646/430-7500
Spain
✉ 150 E 58th Street,
30th Floor
☎ 212/355-4080
UK
✉ 845 3rd Avenue
☎ 212/745-0200

REST ROOMS

● Department stores, hotels, book stores, Time Warner Center, Lincoln Center, Rockefeller Center's underground concourse and Starbucks are the best places to find facilities. Smaller shops and restaurants are often for the use of patrons only.

RADIO AND TELEVISION

● For cable subscribers to Spectrum, NY1 is the main channel serving New York and will give you access to news, weather and travel as well as daily life in the Big Apple.
● WNYC (New York Public Radio) on 93.9 FM and 820 AM has news, culture and music items.
● Many TV shows are filmed in New York, from *Good Morning America* to the *The Daily Show*. Go to nycgo.com/tv-show-tapings for further details on tickets.

SENSIBLE PRECAUTIONS

● Maintain awareness of your surroundings and of other people, and try to look as though you know your way around.
● Avoid the quieter subway lines at night and also certain areas of Brooklyn. Areas of Manhattan once considered unsafe (Alphabet City east of Avenue C, the far west of Midtown, north of about 110th Street and Central Park) are less edgy than they used to be. Still, keep your wits about you in deserted areas.
● Conceal your wallet; keep the fastener of your bag on the inside; and don't flash large amounts of cash or jewelry.

STUDENTS

● An International Student Identity Card (ISIC) is good for reduced admission at many museums, theaters and other attractions.
● Carry the ISIC or some other photo ID card to prove you're a full-time student or over 21.
● Under-25s will find it expensive to rent a car.

VISITOR PASSES

Two visitor passes offer big savings if you're planning to take in multiple attractions:
● New York CityPass ($126 adults, $104 children, citypass.com/new-york) is valid for nine days and covers six top attractions, including the Statue of Liberty, Empire State Building and major museums.
● With the Explorer Pass (from $89 adults, $67 children, smartdestinations.com), you can choose 3, 5, 7 or 11 attractions from a list of 50 top sights and tours; valid for 30 days.

Books and Movies

BOOKS
Non-fiction
- *The Historical Atlas of New York City* by Eric Homberger (2016, 3rd ed.), St Martin's Griffin.
- *Inside the Apple: A Streetwise History of New York City* by Michelle and James Nevius (2009), Free Press.
- *The New York Nobody Knows: Walking 6,000 Miles in the City* (2013), Princeton University Press.
- *The New York Times' Book of New York* (2009), Black Dog & Leventhal Publishers.
- *Five Points* by Tyler Anbinder (2001), Free Press.
- *Humans of New York* by Brandon Stanton (2013), St. Martin's Press.

MOVIES
42nd Street (1933), Lloyd Bacon
King Kong (1933), Merian C. Cooper
Guys and Dolls (1955), Joseph L. Mankiewicz
An Affair to Remember (1957), Leo McCarey
Breakfast at Tiffany's (1961), Blake Edwards
West Side Story (1961), Robert Wise
The French Connection (1971), William Friedkin
Mean Streets (1973), Martin Scorsese
Taxi Driver (1976), Martin Scorsese
Saturday Night Fever (1977), John Badham
Manhattan (1979), Woody Allen
The Cotton Club (1984), Francis Ford Coppola
Desperately Seeking Susan (1985), Susan Seidelman
Do the Right Thing (1989), Spike Lee
When Harry Met Sally (1989), Rob Reiner
A Bronx Tale (1993), Robert De Niro
Requiem for a Dream (2000), Darren Aronofsky
Gangs of New York (2002), Martin Scorsese
The Devil Wears Prada (2006), David Franke
Night at the Museum (2006), Shawn Levy
Julie and Julia (2009), Nora Ephron
The Adjustment Bureau (2011), J.J. Abrams
Birdman (Or the Unexpected Virtue of Ignorance) (2014), Alejandro González Iñárritu
Brooklyn (2015), John Crowley
Fantastic Beasts and Where to Find Them (2016), David Yates
Beach Rats (2017), Eliza Hittman

FICTION
F. Scott Fitzgerald's *The Beautiful and Damned* (1922), John Dos Passos's *Manhattan Transfer* (1925), J.D. Salinger's *The Catcher in the Rye* (1951) and Truman Capote's *Breakfast at Tiffany's* (1958) are all classic reads. Also recommended are Tom Wolfe's *Bonfire of the Vanities* (1987), *The New York Trilogy* (1988) by Paul Auster, and *New York: The Novel* (2010) by Edward Rutherfurd.

Index

We would like to thank the following photographers, companies and picture libraries for their assistance in the preparation of this book.

All images are copyright AA/James Tims, except:

3(iii) Gansevoort Meatpacking NYC Gansevoort, Meatpacking NYC; 4 AA/D Pollack; 6t Nick Wood/Alamy Stock Photo; 6/7b Photolibrary; 7t Photolibrary; 8t AA/C Sawyer; 8b Pablo Valentini/Alamy Stock Photo; 8/9t The Dinex Group Café Boulud NYC by B. Milne; 9bc NYC images/Alamy Stock Photo; 10l AA; 10r Mary Evans Picture Library/ Classic Stock/H. Armstrong Roberts; 11l Mary Evans Picture Library; 11r Lower East Side Tenement Museum Courtesy the Lower East Side Tenement Museum, photography by Keiko Niwa; 16/7t; Michael Matthews /Alamy Stock Photo; 21bl AA/C Sawyer; 22tl Cooper Hewitt Smithsonian Design Museum; 22cl Photo by James Rudrick © 2014 Cooper Hewitt Smithsonian Design Museum; 23 Cooper Hewitt Smithsonian Design Museum; 24 Tetra Images /Alamy Stock Photo; 24/5t AA/C Sawyer; 24/5b AA/Simon McBride; 25t The Ukrainian Museum Courtesy of The Ukrainian Museum; 25b AA/C Sawyer; 30b Patrick Batchelder/Alamy Stock Photo; 30t Sandra Baker/Alamy Stock Photo; 32tr The Frick Collection, New York, The Frick Collection, New York Photo: Michael Bodycomb; 33cr The Frick Collection, New York. The Frick Collection, New York Photo: Galen Lee; 35br Great Northern Food Hall; 38/39 Christian Kober/Robert Harding; 40 Douglas Lander/Alamy Stock Photo; 40/41 Chris A Selby/Alamy Stock Photo; 42/43 Lincoln Center Media Desk Photo Gallery. Photo credit: Mark Bussell Lincoln Center for the Performing Arts; 43t Iñaki Vinaixa for Lincoln Center Media Desk Photo Gallery; 43bl Lincoln Center Media Desk Photo Gallery. Photo credit: Stefan Cohen Lincoln Center for the Performing Arts; 43br Lincoln Center Media Desk Photo Gallery. Photo credit: Mark Bussell Lincoln Center for the Performing Arts; 46 AA/J Tims Chagall®/© ADAGP, Paris and DACS, London 2011 AND © ADAGP, Paris and DACS; London 2011. 46bl Michal Besser/Alamy Stock Photo; 56/7b PACIFIC PRESS/Alamy Stock Photo; 60 Whitney Museum © Whitney Museum/Ed Lederman; 61 Whitney Museum of American Art; 62l John Kellerman/Alamy Stock Photo; 62/63t Christopher Penler/ Alamy Stock Photo; 62/63b Architectural Photographer/Alamy Stock Photo; 63r Gordon Bell/Alamy Stock Photo; 66l American Folk Art Museum American Folk Art Museum; 68 Courtesy of Museum of Arts and Design, Photo by Gustav Liliequist; 69 Photolibrary; 71l Paul Jackson © New Museum of Contemporary Art; 71r Rubin Museum, Peter Aaron.Esto; 72 South Street Seaport; 75 Photolibrary; 79b Spencer Grant /Alamy Stock Photo; 82(vii) John Kellerman/Alamy Stock Photo; 84b AA/World Travel Library/Alamy Stock Photo; 85b Aurora Photos /Alamy Stock Photo; 88(iii) Asia Photopress/Alamy Stock Photo; 88(iv) Robert Nickelsberg/Alamy Stock Photo; 90b AA/Simon McBride; 91 AA/J Tims; 100(ii) AA/C Sawyer; 100(iii) The Frick Collection, New York The Frick Collection, New York; Photo: Michael Bodycomb; 102t American Folk Art Museum American; Folk Art Museum; 102t Matthiola/Alamy Stock Photo; 103b Lincoln Center Media Desk Photo Gallery. Photo credit: Mark Bussell Lincoln Center for the Performing Arts; 107 AA/Simon McBride; 108t Prisma Bildagentur AG/Alamy Stock Photo; 109t Alamy Richard Ellis/Alamy Stock Photo; 113 Julie Larson Maher © WCS; 114 Magpie New York; 116/117b Richard Levine/Alamy Stock Photo; 117mb AA/C Sawyer; 119 ABC Carpet and Home Store; 124 The Mysterious Bookshop, Charles Perry; 128 Prisma Bildagentur AG/Alamy Stock Photo; 128/9t Jon; Arnold Images Ltd/Alamy Stock Photo; 128/9bc Lincoln Center Media Desk; Photo Gallery. Photo credit: Iwan BAA/n Lincoln Center for the Performing Arts; 136 AA/Paul Kenward; 140tc John's Pizzeria; 140bc The Dinex Group Café Boulud NYC by B. Milne; 145 Casa Lever/Nico; 146 Kathy deWitt/ Alamy Stock Photo; 150, 152t Gansevoort; Meatpacking NYC; 152tc Shoreham hotel; 152bc CROSBY STREET/ www.crosbystreethotel.com; 152b The NEW YORK Edition Hotel; 154l CROSBY STREET HOTEL/www.crosbystreethotel.com; 154r Four Seasons Hotels and Resorts/Saylor, Durston; Four Seasons Hotels and Resorts; 156 Gansevoort Meatpacking NYC Gansevoort Meatpacking NYC; 157 Mandarin Oriental, New York; 158 AA/C Sawyer; 159 Shoreham hotel

Every effort has been made to trace the copyright holders, and we apologize in advance for any unintentional omissions or errors. We would be pleased to apply any corrections in a following edition of this publication.

ityPack New York

ublished by AA Publishing, a trading name of AA Media Limited, whose
egistered office is Fanum House, Basing View, Basingstoke, Hampshire
G21 4EA. Registered number 06112600.

AA Media Limited 2019
rst published 1997

ritten by Kate Sekules and Donna Dailey
pdated by Eleanor Berman
eries editor Clare Ashton
esign work Liz Baldin
olour reprographics Ian Little

rinted and bound in China by 1010 Printing Group Limited

CIP catalogue record for this book is available from the British Library.

SBN 978-0-7495-8182-4

he content of this book is believed to be accurate at the time of printing.
ue to its nature the content is likely to vary or change and the publisher is
ot responsible for such change and accordingly is not responsible for the
onsequences of any reliance by the reader on information that has changed.
ny rights that are given to consumers under applicable law are not affected.
pinions expressed are for guidance only and are those of the assessor based
n their experience at the time of review and may differ from the reader's
pinions based on their subsequent experience.

We have tried to ensure accuracy in this guide, but things do change, so please
et us know if you have any comments at travelguides@theAA.com.

A05671
Maps in this title produced from mapping data supplied by Global Mapping,
Brackley, UK © Global Mapping and data available from openstreetmap.org
© under the Open Database License found at opendatacommons.org
Transport map © Communicarta Ltd, UK